QUEEN ANNE'S COUNTY MARYLAND

LAND RECORDS

BOOK THREE: 1738–1747

VOLUMES R.T. B (PP. 202–540) AND R.T. C (PP. 1–266)

COMPILED BY

R. BERNICE LEONARD

HERITAGE BOOKS
2014

HERITAGE BOOKS

AN IMPRINT OF HERITAGE BOOKS, INC.

Books, CDs, and more—Worldwide

For our listing of thousands of titles see our website
at
www.HeritageBooks.com

Published 2014 by
HERITAGE BOOKS, INC.
Publishing Division
5810 Ruatan Street
Berwyn Heights, Md. 20740

Originally published by R. Bernice Leonard: 1994

International Standard Book Numbers
Paperbound: 978-1-58549-293-0
Clothbound: 978-0-7884-9036-1

KENT ISLAND

Kent Point

Love Point

Broad C.

Ferry

Matkuu Place

Ferry

Lookin P.

Elliots P.

Swans I.

Swans P.

Reed I.

2 Fath.

Kitutis & Croos.

Bach

Winds Pound

Wye River

Bennetts Point

S.Michaels R.

O-s River

Waymanols C.

Queens Town

Coursey Point

Piney Point

Gray Inlet C.

Spaniards Point

Reed C.

Corsica C.

Lankfords Bay

Comogy's Point

Old Town Ferry

Bach C.

Ogle Town

Chester

S.E. Branch

Ch

Septenk is Navigable with Shallops to the tides about 7 Miles within Delaware Colony.

QUEEN ANN'S COUNTY LAND RECORDS

CONTENTS - BOOK THREE

****

ABOUT THE INDEXES

    References are to the page numbers of the original
records, shown in the left-hand margins of this book.

THE ORIGIN OF QUEEN ANN'S COUNTY

Since Talbot County was the parent of Queen Ann's County, it behooves us to touch briefly on it's origin at the beginning.

The date on which Talbot County was formally established has never come to light; it may have been as early as 1658 when surveyors began to lay out land on the eastern side of the Chesapeake Bay en masse. The name appears with certainty in a charge made by the General Assembly to the interim Sheriff, 18 February 1661. At this time and during the ensuing years, Talbot extended northward to the Chester River and there are evidences that there were tracts on the northern side of the river held by colonists who were under the jurisdiction of the Talbot County court. Poplar Island, lying in the Chesapeake Bay to the westward of Talbot, had been given to Kent (Island) County in 1657 but must have been in the territory laid out for Talbot County, for on 4 June 1671, Philip Calvert ordered that the land on the northeast side of Chester River - "as far as the bounds of Talbot County were formerly - shall now be added to Kent County, as also Poplars Island. And, I do require that the Sheriff of Talbot County not to collect any quit rents from the inhabitants living there." Even so, uncertainty prevailed in some minds, for in a survey made 5 February 1684, for a parcel of land called "Craycroft's Purchase," the tract is described as lying in Talbot County at the head of the Gunpowder River! The eastern border of Talbot, subject of dispute for decades, seems to been acknowledged by those landowners in what is now the First Election District of Queen Ann's County, for as late as 1740, "an old poplar tree - the southwest corner of Governour Penn's Mannor of Pensilvania," was a landmark. In 1695 Kent Island was given to Talbot, a decision of unpopularity to many of the settlers.

Forty-five years after Talbot County had become a part of Maryland history, the settlements along the Chester River, the Tuckahoe and Great Choptank, had grown considerably. The County Courthouse, located at Yorke on a tributary of Wye River called Skipton Creek, was a long journey from Head of Chester (now Millington in Queen Ann's County) and equally so for those plantation owners living east of Tuckahoe Creek on St. Jones' Path (the road from Tuckahoe to St. Jones, now Dover, Delaware). The Governor and Council of the Province were beseiged with petitions from the inhabitants of both Talbot and Kent Counties for a more equitable access to the seat of Justice. So, at the session of Assembly beginning 2 April 1706, the petitions having been read and under consideration for two years, it was decided to divide Talbot County into two parts, the new county so formed to be called QUEEN ANN'S COUNTY, after Queen Anne, consort of King James I of England. Two new courthouses were then needed so commissioners were appointed to arrange for the surveys and purchase of two acres of land for the site of each. That selected for Queen Ann's was on the plantation of John Hawkins on Coursey's Creek; where the county seat was to be called QUEENS TOWN. Here the first county courthouse was erected before 1710.

The Levy List presented at the November 1706 term of Talbot County Court reveals the charges and payments made for the expense of dividing the county. Paid in tobacco at the rate of eighty pounds per day: "for canoing to divide ye county," were Daniel Sherwood (3); John Hawkins (3); Richard Tilghman (3); William Turlo (1); Philemon Hemsley (2); Matthew Tilghman Ward (4); John Coppedge (2); William Elliott (2); Valentine Carter (2); William Browne (2); Robert Goldsborough (1). Ralph Stevenson, Innkeeper, received 920 pounds of tobacco "for the expenses of those persons at their first meeting in consulting about dividing ye county."

William Turbutt, Surveyor, was paid 2,500 pounds of tobacco "for running out ye divisional line;" Robert Grundy received 320 "for four days attendance in dividing ye county" and four hundred pounds more "for accomodating all those persons which were about ye same." Chain carriers were paid twenty-five pounds of tobacco per day and Robert Ungle collected 480 pounds "for several chain carriers about ye divisional line;" while the following made claims in person: William Martin (1); William Cooper (4); James London (4); John Hall (1); William Draper (1); David Arey (3); Joseph Arey (3); John Keld (3). At 80 pounds of tobacco per day, John Dawson (2); Thomas Emerson (5); Robert Grundy (2) and James Lloyd (6), were paid "for attendance about dividing ye county."

In the same levy, a payment of 1,200 pounds of tobacco was made to Col. Thomas Smith, Speaker of The House "for a Bill for ye division of Kent and Queen Ann's Counties;" and 600 pounds paid to William Taylard for the same.

Once the divisions were made, the Assembly set the court dates as the first Tuesday in February, April, July, September, October and December. Extant records show sessions of court held in every month in later years. At least two Justices were required to be present during each session, they to have power to determine the length of time needed to conduct the court's business.

The first Clerk of Court for Queen Ann's County was Evan Thomas (E.T.). The second, beginning in 1714, was James Knowles (I.K.); the third was Richard Tilghman (R.T.).

****

BIBLIOGRAPHY

Tavern In The Town - Leonard, 1992
The County Courthouses of Maryland - Radoff, 1960
Queen Anne's County, Maryland - Emory, 1886-7
Old Kent - Hanson, 1876
The Counties of Maryland - Matthews, 1907
Judgments (County Court Records) - Maryland State Archives

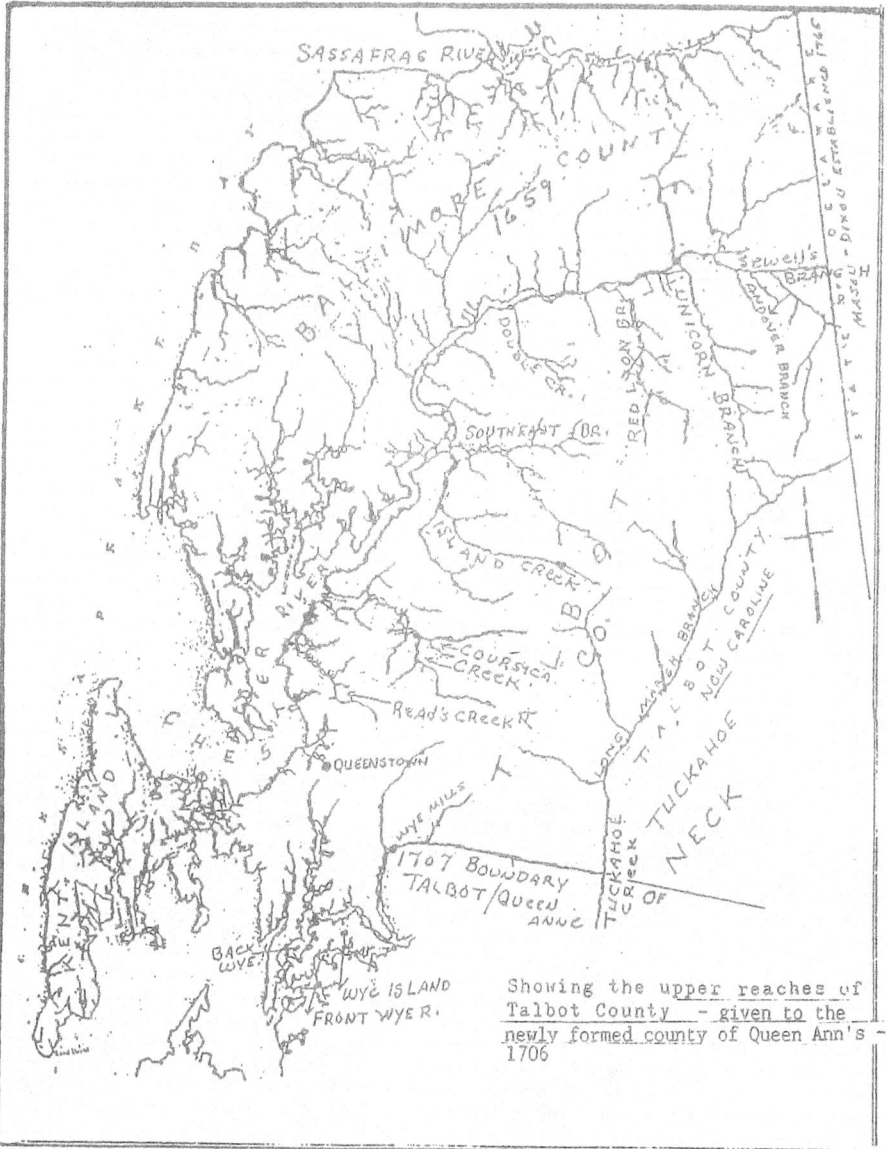

Showing the upper reaches of Talbot County — given to the newly formed county of Queen Ann's — 1706

QUEEN ANNE COUNTY LAND RECORDS - R. T. B 1737 - 1743

The reconstructed Courthouse at Queenstown as it looks today. The entrance to the older wooden section on the right is at the rear; the brick section on the left was added at a later date to the original building.

Page
202. 16 September 1738 - 21 December 1738 William Bennett, Jr., Planter, to Nicholas Brodaway, Planter - consideration 2,500 pounds of tobacco - 60 acres, part of "Anthorpe," lying near a place called Wills Hole and intersecting "Churnell's Neck" and "Whitehall." Wits: A. Thompson, James Brown. Acknowledged before A. Thompson and H. Wells.

203. 16 January 1738 Chattel mortgage given by Josiah Coleman, Innholder, to Richard Tilghman, Esquire. For the consideration of ₺34.13.11, four featherbeds, bedsteads and furniture; two new country made bedticks; four iron pots; two dozen pewter plates; four pewter basons; six pewter dishes; ten dozen pewter spoons; a black horse called "Blaze;" a sorrel horse called "Bale;" a large, grey, fleabitten mare called "Bonny;" two large chests; a small walnut desk and stand; two dozen rush chairs; six silver teaspoons, tongs and strainer; four shoats and four breeding sows; Coleman to make payment before 24 August next. Wits: C. Downes, R. Tilghman, Jr.

204. 4 October 1738 - 22 January 1738 William Coursey, Gentleman, to Rachell Clayton, Gentlewoman - a gift in recognition of their intended marriage - 800 acres of land, all of "Cheston" on Wye River; also 290 acres adjoining, part of "Coursey upon Wye," on Wye River, for and during her natural life. Wits: T. H. Wright, Tho. Wilkinson.

204. 30 October 1738 - 25 January 1738 John Ball of Kent County (Md.) and Jane his wife, to James Bell - consideration ₺20 paper money of Maryland - 120 acres in Tuckahoe Neck, part of "Turner's Plains Addition." Acknowledged before Charles Hynson and Ebenezar Blakiston, certified as Justices of the Peace by James Smith, Clerk of Kent County. Alienation fine, four shillings, ten pence sterling.

206. 27 November 1738 - 25 January 1738 Joshua Clarke of Talbot County, Carpenter, to Walter Lane, Blacksmith - consideration 7,700 pounds of tobacco - 110 acres, part of "Stevens' Fields" - on the east side of Tuckahoe Creek. Wits: Charles Downes, Thomas Wilkinson. Alienation fine, two shillings, two pence sterling.

207. 25 January 1738 Richard Tilghman, Jr. to James Hicks - receipt for eight shillings sterling, alienation fine for the deed recorded on pages 194 and 195.

207. 14 FEbruary 1738 - 1 March 1738 Nicholas Brodaway, Planter, and Anne his wife, to William Ratcliffe - consideration 2,000 pounds of tobacco - 18 acres, part of "White Hall," adjoining "Spread Eagle." Wits: A. Thompson, Thomas Wilkinson, before the deed was acknowledged. A. Thompson and Christopher Wilkinson witnessed the receipt given by Brodaway to Ratcliffe. Alienation fine, nine pence sterling.

208. 7 February 1738 - 8 March 1738 David Harrington, Planter, from Neriah Jones, Innholder - in consideration of Ŀ45 current - 150 acres on Beaverdam Branch called "Beaverdam Addition." Wits: Ambrose Wright, Thomas Pryor. Harrington acknowledged before C. Downes and Thomas Wilkinson.

210. 8 February 1738 - 27 March 1739 William Roberts to John Hadley - in consideration of 3,000 pounds of tobacco - 50 acres on the Beaverdam Branch in ye Forrest of Choptank, called "Skinner's Pleasure." Wits: Humphery Wells and Grundy Pemberton. Alienation fine, two shillings sterling paid to Richard Tilghman, Jr.

211. 27 March 1739 Robert Crump to Humphery Wells, Gentleman - consideration 3,000 pounds of tobacco - 50 acres called "Crump's Fancy," near the head of the Long Marsh, on the northeast side of the path that goes to Pocky and so to ye Horse Head being .ye head of a great marsh called Tappahanna Marsh. Wits: C. Downes, J. Wickes. Alienation fine, two shillings sterling.

212. 14 March 1739 - 27 March 1739 Ernault Hawkins and Jane his wife, daughter and heir at law of Mary Cole, deceased, to John Collins - consideration 3,000 pounds of tobacco - 290 acres, "Smith's Range Addition," lying in Talbot County but now in Queen Ann's, on the Southeast Branch of Chester River - adjoining "Ripley," formerly laid out for Stephen Tully and a parcel formerly laid out for Thomas Collins; and "Smith's Range." Ernault and Jane (she being first privately examined) acknowledged before C. Downes and T. Wilkinson.

214. 28 March 1739 At a Sessions of Goal Delivery held for County Cornwall 1 August last, William Basely and John Edgers were convicted of felony and sentenced to be transported to the American colonies for a term of seven years. At the General Quarter Sessions held at Bodwyn in the said county, 3 October last, Agnes Cloore, singlewoman, was convicted and sentenced to a term of seven years in the colonies and according to the laws, Hugh Pypers and Edward Bennett, Esquires, two

214. Justices of the Peace, contracted with George Buck of Bideford for their transportation which he agreed to do within three months; the contract witnessed by Daniel Welland and George Conner. Buck assigned the contract to Capt. Robert Maine of the ship, "Amity" before John Biseck and Thomas Smith.

215. 30 March 1739 John Dempster, Planter, to William Ginniss of Chestertown, Mariner - in consideration pf ₤5 current money - Lot Number Fifteen in Kings Town. Wits: William Hopper, John Collins. Acknowledged before T. H. Wright and Associates.

216. 20 February 1738 - 18 April 1739 Albert Johnson, Planter, to John Johnson, Jr., Planter - in compliance with the will of his father, Henry Johnson and the natural love and affection he hath for his brother - 80 acres, part of "Notlar's Delight," lying on the north side of Hambleton's Branch - beginning at a bounded tree of "Dangerfield," laid out for William Bishop; a parcel laid out for Henry Denton called "Clowdent;" and "Barton," laid out for William Hackett. Wits: Augustine Thompson, Elizabeth Thompson. James Horsley witnessed Albert Johnson's receipt to John Johnson for five shillings. Alienation fine, three shillings, two pence sterling.

217. 18 April 1739 Richard Tilghman, Jr. to John Collins - receipt for eleven shillings, seven pence sterling, alienation fine for a deed recorded on folios 212, 213 and 214.

217. 19 April 1739 Richard Tilghman, Jr. to William Shepherd - receipt for one pence sterling, alienation fine of lott Number Eleven in Kings Town, from John Dempster.

217. 19 April 1739 William Shepard, Yoeman, and Catherine his wife, to John Nevill, Planter - consideration ₤50 current and 3,000 pounds of tobacco - part of a lot adjoining Number Eleven in Kings Town. William and Catherine (she being first privately examined) acknowledged their deed before William Jumpe and Thomas Wilkinson. Alienation fine, one pence sterling, paid to Richard Tilghman, Jr.

220. 20 April 1739 John Hawkins, Gentleman, to Archibald Greenfield, Mariner - consideration ₤20 current - a house and lot Numbered Two, in Ogletown. Wits: G. Pemberton, John Brown.

221. 23 April 1739 - 30 April 1739 John Hawkins, Jr., Gentleman, and Sarah his wife, to James Hollyday, Esquire - consideration ₤90 current money - about 90 acres, part of "Macklinborough," now in the occupation of Edward Brown and Mary his wife, mother of the said Sarah, whereon they now dwell - adjoining such part as was sold to Hollyday, 4 February 1734; another part on 31 December 1737; and on the northeast by part of the dwelling plantation of John Hawkins, father to the said John; on the northwest by the Chester River. John and Sarah acknowledged before Robert Loyd and James Copson, Justices of the Provincial Court. Alienation fine, one shilling, nine pence sterling.

223. 20 November 1738 - 30 April 1739 George Gale and John Gale of Somerset County (Md.), Merchants, to William Hewbanks - consideration
£14 current - 140 acres, part of "Ratcliff," adjoining William Mountaque's part and "Old Town." Wits: Levin Gale, Thomas Gillis. Acknowledged before Levin Gale, Justice of the Provincial Court. Alienation fine, five shillings, eight pence sterling.

224. 20 November 1738 - 30 April 1739 George Gale and John Gale, Merchants, to William Mounticue - consideration £14 current - 140 acres,
part of "Ratcliff," conveyed to them by an Act of Assembly impower-
ing commissioners to sell the lands of Samuel Groome the elder, and
Samuel Groome, the younger.

225. 5 May 1739 - 2 June 1739 Francis Watson of Dorchester County, Planter, and Elizabeth his wife, to Thomas Mooth, Planter - consideration 3,375 pounds of tobacco - 50 acres, part of "Watson's Delight,"
on the Beaverdam Marsh - beginning at a tree of "Skinner's Expecta-
tion" - also 25 acres, one-quarter of "Friendship," surveyed for
William Parsons, lying on the east side of the marsh and near "Watson's Delight." Wits: Henry Hooper, John Hodson. Acknowledged before Henry Hooper, Justice of the Provincial Court. Alienation fine,
three shillings sterling, paid to Richard Tilghman, Jr.

227. 6 June 1739 At the General Quarter Sessions held at Brewton, County Somerset (Eng.), 11 April 1738 before Abraham Gapper, Seargant at
at law; Thomas Prouse; James Strode; Thomas Coward and Thomas Baynard, Esquires and others, their fellow Justices, Barnard Hollard
was convicted of felony and sentenced to the American colonies for
a term of seven years; Thomas Carew, Edward Dyke, Adam Martin, George
Speke of Dillington, George Speke of Currywell, John Roebard and
Henry Palmer, Esquires, seven of His Majestie's Justices, or any two
of them were appointed to contract for the transportation of the
felons. At the General Quarter Sessions held at Bridgewater for
Somerset County on Tuesday, 11 July 1738 before Edward Dyke, Andrew
Crosse, Thomas Carew, John Gunston, George Biss and Davidge Gould,
Esquires and fellow Justices, William Harris, John Quick, John Sut-
ton als Andrews, William Manning and John Palmer were convicted and
ordered to be transported; the seven last named Justices again were
appointed to arrange for their transportation. At the General Quarter Sessions held at Taunton, County Somerset, Tuesday 3 October
1738 before Thomas Carew, Esq., Sir William Wyndham, Abraham Gapper,
Esq., Sgt. at Law, Thomas Hayward, John Gunston and Adam Martin, Esquires, George Slocombe, Thomas Slape and Richard Shelton, convicted
of felony, were ordered to be transported to the colonies for seven
years. This same court nominated Thomas Carew, Sir William Wyndham,
and Sir John Trevelyan, Baronets; Edward Dyke, Adam Martin, George
Speke and Cannon Southey, Esquires, or any two, to make a contract
with someone for transportation of the felons; the said contractor
required to make a bond. Arrangements were made with Etheldred Davy
of the City of Exon, Merchant, 21 November 1738, by Adam Martin and
George Speke. John Churchill and John Butcher witnessed the signa-
ture of Adam Martin; Henry Hoyt and William Hoyt for George Speke.

229. 6 June 1739 At the last Sessions of Goal Delivery held at the Castle of Exon, County of Devon (Eng.), Monday 24 July last, George
Gent, John Woodward and Richard Dare, convicted of felony, were sentenced to be transported to Maryland or any other of the American
colonies - there to serve for a term of seven years. At a former
session, Richard Webb, Richard Perkins, Joseph Crabb, James Binney
and James Stewart were similarly convicted and sentenced. Sir
George Chudleigh, Francis Fullford, Esq., Samuel Cruwys, Esq., Richard Beavis, Esq., Joseph Taylor, Esq., John Gibbs, Esq., Caleb Juglet, Esq., George Buck, Esq., Thomas Saltern, Esq., Joseph Benson,
Esq., and the Rev. Chichester Wrey, Clerk, twelve Justices of the
peace, or any two, were appointed to contract and receive a bond
from some person to transport the felons, which was carried out by
Caleb Juglet and Richard Beavis. Etheldred Davy of the City of Exon, Esquire, agreed to remove the prisoners within three months of
date, 29 December 1738. Thomas Ley and John Sampson witnessed for
Juglet; Simon Pridham and John Mayne for Beavis.

231. 6 June 1739 At the Gaol Delivery Sessions held at Bridgewater, County of Somerset (Eng.), Tuesday 8 August before Sir John Fortescue
Aland, Knight, and Sir William Thomson, Knight, Richard Stokes and
Robert Jones were convicted of felony and sentenced to the American
colonies for seven years; at a former session, Thomas Commons, convicted of burglary, was sentenced for a term of fourteen years.
Sir William Wyndham, Sir John Trevelyan, Thomas Carew, Esq., Cannon
Southey, Esq., Edward Dyson, Esq., and Adam Martin, Esq., or any two
of them, were appointed to arrange for their transportation. Southey
and Martin contracted with Etheldred Davy to remove the convicts
within three months of date, 6 December 1738. Elizabeth Goodfellow
and Richard Cudland, Jr. witnessed for Southey; John Churchill and
John Butcher for Martin.

232. 6 June 1739 At the last Quarter Sessions held at the Castle of Exon,
County of Devon (Eng.), on 11 July last, John Pargilly, George Rad-
ford, John Williams, Phillipa Lamman, Sarah Sommers and Catherine
Pulsevir were convicted of felony and sentenced for a term of seven
years; Richard Beavis, Richard Duke and Caleb Juglett, Esquires,
appointed to contract with some person, with security, for the transportation of the felons. Etheldred Davy, County of Exon, Merchant,
signed the contract, 18 July 1738; John Hayman and John Haeve witnessed for Richard Beavis, John Parratt and John Haeve for Duke.

233. 17 June 1739 - 18 June 1739 Joshua Clark of Talbot County, Carpenter, to Henry Cliffe, Planter - consideration 5,450 pounds of tobacco - 78 acres of land, part of "Stevens Fields," lying on the east
side of Tuckahoe Creek. Wits: N. Wright, Anthony Roe. Acknowledged
before Thomas H. Wright and J. Wickes.

234. 19 June 1739 Richard Tilghman to John Elliott - receipt for six
shillings, two pence, half penny sterling, alienation fine for deed
recorded on folios 166 and 167.

234. 27 December 1738 - 10 July 1739 Samuel Harris of Marblehead, County of Essex (Eng.), Trader, to Richard James of Marblehead, Mariner, Power of Attorney to represent him in the colonies on all accounts. 28 December 1738 Marblehead - Samuel Harris acknowledged his Power of Attorney before Joshua Rue, Justice of the Peace.

235. 5 July 1739 - 24 July 1739 James Cook, Taylor, to Jacob Boon, Planter - consideration 15,000 pounds of tobacco - mortgage on all of his lands, goods and chattels - due on or before 4 July next. Wits: R. N. Wright, Nathan Wright. Acknowledged before William Ratcliffe and James Brown.

235. 24 July 1739 Richard Tilghman to David Harrington - receipt for one shilling sterling, alienation fine for a deed recorded on folios 208, 209, and 210.

235. 24 July 1739 - 25 July 1739 Andrew Jordan, Planter, and Margreat his wife, to John Stout, Planter - consideration 3,000 pounds of tobacco - part of "Cole Rain," formerly laid out for John Pitt of Talbot County - lying on Tuckahoe Creek and adjoining part now in the possession of Richard Ross; containing 103 acres. Margreat Jordan relinquished her dower. John and 'Margrett' acknowledged before William Ratcliffe and James Brown, she being first privately examined. Alienation fine, two shillings, 3 farthings sterling.

238. 25 July 1739 - 27 July 1739 Joshua Clark of Talbot County, Carpenter, to William Banning, Planter - consideration 3,000 pounds of tobacco - 50 acres called "Clark's Venture," lying at the head of Gunnery's Branch - adjoining "Lyford;" and "Sewall's Manor," now in possession of Richard Bennett, Esquire. Wits: G. Pemberton, George Baynard. Acknowledged before William Ratcliffe and J. Wickes. Alienation fine, two shillings sterling paid to Richard Tilghman.

239. 25 July 1739 - 29 August 1739 William Bishop, Gentleman, to Daniel McClean, Cordwainer - nine-year lease beginning 1 January next, of the plantation where Robert Smith lived upon - lying on the north side of Coursey's Creek in Spaniard's Neck; the yearly rent, 1,000 pounds of tobacco. Acknowledged before Thomas H. Wright and Joseph Sudler.

240. 15 September 1737 - 29 August 1739 Peter Frome, Blacksmith, to Solomon Clayton, Gentleman - consideration ₤20 current gold and ₤14 current paper money of Maryland - a negro woman slave named "Nann," and a negro boy slave named "Cesar" - slaves for life. Wits: William Bishop, John Maffett.
15 August 1739 Solomon Clayton to his son Edward Clayton - gift of the above slaves. Wits: Nat. Cleave, Thos. Wilkinson.

240. 30 August 1739 Archable Douglis to Thomas Owens - consideration 4,000 pounds of tobacco - 85 acres of land, part of "Kendall." Wits: Thomas H. WRight, James Brown. Alienation fine, three shillings, five pence sterling.

242. 9 June 1739 - 31 August 1739   Thomas Hynson, Jr., Gentleman, Kent
County in Maryland, and Isabella his wife; Hanse Hanson of the same
county, Planter, and Sarah his wife to John Dempster, Planter - 498
acres of land called "Poplar Hill," lying near the mouth of Fishing
Creek. Mortgaged by Daniel Pearce of Kent County, father of the
said Isabella and Sarah, for 40,000 pounds of tobacco, 19 March 1723.
Pearce afterwards died leaving a son Andrew, who soon after died,
and Isabella and Sarah, his sisters, who are now heirs at law. Wits:
B. Hands, Thomas Williams, Jr., Justices of the Peace for Kent County; certified by James Smith, Clerk of Kent County. Alienation fine,
nine shillings, eleven pence, one-half penny sterling.

244. 5 July 1739 - 6 September 1739   John Baynard, Planter, to John Woot-
ters, Planter - consideration 3,500 pounds of tobacco - 50 acres,
part of "Jumpe's Choice," lying in the fork between Tuckahoe Creek
and Choptank River, on St. Jones's Path. Wits: J. Wickes, William
Ratcliffe. Alienation fine two shillings sterling.

246. 20 September 1739   Richard Tilghman to Henry Cliffe - receipt for
one shilling, six pence, three farthings, for the deed on folios
233 and 234.

246. 15 October 1739 - 1 November 1739   William and Rebecca Watson to
Thomas Wyatt - consideration 4,000 pounds of tobacco - 50 acres
called "Watson's Chance," in the Long Neck, west side of Maple Swamp.
William and Rebecca, she being first privately examined, acknowledged before William Ratcliffe and James Brown. Alienation fine, two
shillings sterling.

248. 10 October 1739 - 9 November 1739   William Shepherd of Kent County
on Delaware, late of Queen Anns County, Planter, and Catherine his
wife, to John Dempster - consideration £84 current money and 6,250
pounds of tobacco - 150 acres, the remaining part of "Shepherd's
Fortune," on Jones's Creek - adjoining "Barefield." William and
Catherine acknowledged before Thomas Hynson Wright and James Brown,
she being first privately examined. Alienation fine, six shillings
sterling paid to Richard Tilghman.

249. 16 November 1739 - 27 November 1739   Ernault Hawkins, Gentleman, and
Jane his wife, daughter of Mary Cole, Widow, deceast, to William
Simpson, Weaver - consideration 4,000 pounds of tobacco - land patented to Robert Smith, 17 June 1679 - two parcels on the southwest
branch of Island Creek; one, part of "Larrington," 125 acres; the
other part of a tract laid out for one Juniper als Jenifer and containing 100 acres. On 16 March 1700 Robert Smith conveyed to Renatus Smith and heirs recorded in S.W. No. H f.101 sig. pr. John Dowdall, Clk. Renatus Smith willed to his daughter Mary Cole and her
heirs. Ernault and Jane (she being first privately examined out of
his hearing) acknowledged their deed before William Ratcliffe and
James Brown. Alienation fine, four shillings, sterling.

252. 28 November 1739 John Leonard, Planter, to Risdon Bozman - consideration 5,000 pounds of tobacco - 100 acres, "Millford," formerly in Talbot, now in Queen Ann's County - on the east side of Tuckahoe Creek. John acknowledged before William Ratcliffe and Joseph Sudler. Alienation fine, four shillings sterling.

253. 30 November 1739 Thomas Hynson Wright to his daughter Anne, wife of Edward Oldham of Talbot County - a gift of love and affection - 470 acres, part of "Exchange," lying between the branches of Island Creek. Also 60 acres, part of "Exchange." Also part of "Providence," containing 300 acres, lying east of 200 acres sold to Thomas Peacock & Betts (100 acres not yet conveyed). Wits: John Brown, Nathan Wright. Acknowledged before Robert Norrest Wright and Thomas Wilkinson. Alienation fine, ₤1.13. 2½ sterling, paid to Richard Tilghman.

254. 18 November 1739 - 30 November 1739 Thomas Wilkinson, Gentleman, to Alexander King, Weaver - lease of part of "Hitt or Miss," 50 acres of land adjoining George Mattershaw's land; "Barbathus Hall" and a path that leads from Thomas Wilkinson's to Joseph Tryall's, then to the main road that leads from Thomas Dodd's to Chester Church. Lease to begin from 10 January next for a period of nine years - the yearly rent ₤3 or else tobacco on the market priced at two shillings sterling; with liberty of timber for repairing. Wits: Thomas Dodd, Jr., Christopher Wilkinson.

255. 30 November 1739 - 1 December 1739 John Earle, Gentleman, to Archibald Greenfield, Mariner - consideration ₤8 current - Lot Number Twenty-five in Ogletown. Acknowledged before William Ratcliffe and James Brown. Alienation fine, one pence sterling.

256. 4 December 1739 Elizabeth Hawkins, Gentlewoman, to her friend and kinswoman, Sarah, wife of John Emory, Jr. - a gift of love - one negro girl called "Carige(?)". Acknowledged before William Jumpe and William Ratcliffe.

257. 22 November 1739 - 6 December 1739 Elizabeth Hawkins, Widow and relict of Col. Ernault Hawkins, to Richard Bennett, Merchant - consideration ₤30 sterling - part of "The Wading Place Marshes," purchased by John Hawkins, father of Ernault Hawkins, from Thomas Jackson and by Thomas Jackson from William Hempstead for 200 acres - on Broad Cove and Marshy Creek; the Wading Place or Narrows and the Eastern Bay. Wits: John Beck, John Loockerman, Jr. Elizabeth acknowledged before William Jumpe and William Ratcliffe. Alienation fine, four shillings sterling.

259. 12 November 1739 - 6 December 1739 Susannah Gallaspie, Widow, the surviving child and heir at law of Isaac Harris, late of Kent Island, deceased, to Thomas Hynson Wright, Gentleman - consideration ₤30 current - all of her right to 200 acres of land, part of "Guilford," lying near the branches of Corsica Creek; which her deceased father, Isaac Harris, bought of Solomon Wright. Wits: Thomas Maclannahan, Vincent Vanderford. Acknowledged before R. N. Wright and T. Wilk'n.

260. 26 November 1739 - 6 December 1739 Mary Wright, Widow, to her sons
Solomon Wright and Solomon Coursey Wright - a gift of love - two
negroes, one called "Harry," the other, "Dafney" and her issue if
born before sons attain the age of twenty-one or at their day of marriage. Son Solomon to have first choice, Mary reserving their use
until such time. Wits: Nathan Wright, Mary Ann Wright. Acknowledged before Thomas Hynson Wright.

260. 8 December 1739 - 10 December 1739 Mary Turbutt, Singlewoman, to
John Emory, Jr. - in consideration of a marriage about to take place
between herself and Nathan Wright and the further sum of five shillings - conveys in trust for the issue of Nathan and herself, these
negroes: "Yorkshire," "Moll, the elder," "Judy, the elder," "Rachell,"
"Phyllis, the younger," "David," "Rebecca" and "Vincent," son of
"Judy," the elder; reserving to herself the increase, she to have
use of the slaves during her natural life. Acknowledged before
William Ratcliffe and James Brown.

262. 15 October 1739 - 17 December 1739 William Watson and Rebecca his
wife, to Trustom Thomas - consideration 5,000 pounds of tobacco -
50 acres called "Grubby Neck," lying in the Long Neck - near ye Beaver Dam Marsh. William and Rebecca, she being first privately examined, acknowledged before William Ratcliffe and James Brown. Alienation fine, two shillings, sterling.

264. 1 December 1739 - 18 December 1739 Benjamin Harbert, Planter, to
John Hawkins and William Watson, his securities in an action against
him at the suit of one Thomas Stanton - two featherbeds with furni-
ture; two horses; one mare; two cows; a servant woman named Margaret
Farrand. Wits: Thomas Wilkinson, John Davis. Acknowledged before
Robert Norrest Wright and Thomas Wilkinson.

264. 12 December 1739 - 24 January 1739 Richard Scotten and Mary his
wife, to Joseph Sudler, Merchant - consideration £13 current - 15
acres, part of "Davenishes Chance," on Unicorn Branch and adjoining
"Sledmar." Richard and Mary (she being first privately examined)
acknowledged before William Ratcliffe and James Brown. Alienation
fine, seven pence half-penny sterling paid to Richard Tilghman.

266. 29 December 1739 - 2 February 1739 Elizabeth Hawkins, Relict and
devisee of Ernault Hawkins; Ernault Hawkins and Jane his wife, daughter of Mary Cole, daughter of Renatus Smith, to Thomas Hynson Wright -
consideration 15,000 pounds of tobacco and a release from Wright of
his right and claim against Hawkins to part of "Conquest" that shall
happen to be included between the west line of "Bishop's Addition"
and "Smith's Mistake" (being) a resurvey of "Coursey's Point," and a
cove called Bishop's Cove - conveys "Brampton's Addition," 314 acres
of land sometimes called "Bishop's Addition" - lying on the north
side of Corsica Creek. Wits: John Hawkins, Robert N. Wright. Acknowledged before Robert N. Wright and Thomas Wilkinson. Alienation
fine, twelve shillings, seven pence sterling.

268. 7 February 1739 William Cole of Talbot County, Wheelright, to his
      son, John Cole, and Anna his wife - a gift of love - 150 acres at
      the head of Wye River called "Cole's Endeavour" - near "Hemsley's
      Arcadia" - given to John and his heirs, male and female and in fail-
      ure of such, Anna to have during her widowhood; if she remarries
      then his daughter Rebeckah Cole and her heirs to inherit and in fail-
      ure of such then to his son James Cole and his heirs forever. Ack-
      nowledged before R. N. Wright and T. Wilkinson.

269. 18 December 1739 - 7 February 1739 John Harris, Planter, to Sarah
      Benton his daughter and now wife of Vincent Benton - a gift of love
      and affection - the tenement whereon Vincent Benton now dwells, part
      of the "Contention" on the south side of Red Lyon Branch and con-
      taining 50 acres. For want of issue of Sarah, her next heir at law
      by blood to inherit. Acknowledged before William Ratcliffe and
      James Brown. Alienation fine, two shillings sterling.

270. 20 September 1739 - 5 March 1739 David Berry, Planter, and Mary his
      wife, to Andrew McKittrick, M.D. - consideration 7,000 pounds of to-
      bacco - 150 acres, one-half of "Crump's Forrest," lying on the east
      side of the southwest branch of Island Creek. Sig: "Barry."
      Daniel and Mary (she being first privately examined) acknowledged
      before William Ratcliffe and James Brown. Alienation fine, six shil-
      lings sterling paid to Richard Tilghman.

272. 29 October 1739 - 25 March 1740 Richard Lee and Jane his wife, to
      William Cannon - consideration 5,500 pounds of tobacco - 200 acres,
      part of "Content" - lying on Tuckahoe Creek and late in possession
      of Thomas Gaul, deceased. William Campbell, Jr. and William Rat-
      cliffe witnessed Lee's receipt to Cannon. Richard and Jane (she
      being first privately examined) acknowledged before William Ratcliffe
      and James Brown.

274. 19 February 1739 - 26 March 1740 Thomas Price to Richard Lee and
      Jane his wife - lease for part of "Conclusion," 75 acres next to
      Smith's Branch; from 25 December last for a term of fourteen years.
      Paying a yearly rent of 500 pounds of tobacco for the first seven
      years and 600 pounds of tobacco for the other seven. Lee to build
      a good dwelling house, 20 x 16 feet, 8 feet between sill and plate;
      bastard frame to be done workmanlike; all of smooth boards, only
      Thomas Price to find nails. Lee also to plant 100 apple trees, to
      be got by Lee and planted where Price shall think fitt. Price oblig-
      es to find nails and timber to build a tobacco house, 30 x 20 feet,
      10 feet between sill and plate, bastard frame, as also to pay a work-
      man for compleating the building and finish it in two years; Lee to
      have a tobacco house of like dimensions which is on the plantation
      where James Moody dwells. Richard Lee and Jane to have as much char-
      red ground as will contain 20,000 tobacco plants, on the southeast
      side of the plantation where Moody lives. Wits: N. Wright, Edw.
      Wright. Price acknowledged before R. N. Wright and W. Ratcliffe.

275. 26 March 1740 James Berwick, Planter, and Mary his wife, to Henry
      Casson, Merchant - consideration 7,000 pounds of tobacco - 124 acres,
      part of "Large Range Addition," bought of Thomas Fisher, heir at law
      to Richard Fisher, deceased - lying on the east side of Tuckahoe
      Creek and on the south side of William Jumpe's dwelling plantation;
      near the main road that goes from Tuckahoe Bridge to ye head of Chop-
      tank. James and Mary (she being first privately examined) acknow-
      ledged their deed before Robert Norrest Wright and William Ratcliffe.
      Alienation fine, two shillings, eleven pence sterling paid to Rich-
      ard Tilghman.

277. 8 February 1739 - 26 March 1740 John Emory, Planter, and Ann his
      wife, to Joseph Merchant, Planter - consideration 4,000 pounds of
      tobacco - 75 acres of land called "Jack's Purchase," adjoining the
      land called the "Bee Tree," formerly laid out for John Emory. Wits:
      David Register, William Emory, Jr. John and Ann (she being first
      privately examined) acknowledged before Thomas H. Wright and Joseph
      Wickes. Alienation fine, three shillings sterling.

279. 11 February 1739 - 3 April 1740 George Vanderford and Elinor his
      wife, to John Hayes, Jr., Planter - consideration 8,000 pounds of to-
      bacco - 47 acres, part of "Brotherhood," formerly called "Dispute" -
      lying on Hambleton's Branch, adjoining "Outrange." Patented by Ed-
      ward Wright and sold to George Vanderford and Sarah his wife, 2 Sep-
      tember 1729. George and Elinor (she being first privately examined)
      acknowledged before James Brown and William Ratcliffe. Alienation
      fine, one shilling, eleven pence sterling.

281. 29 December 1739 - 10 April 1740 Thomas Hynson Wright to Ernault
      Hawkins and Jane his wife - in consideration of a release of "Bramp-
      ton's Addition" or "Bishop's Addition" on the east side of Bishop's
      Cove whereon Ernault Hawkins now dwells - conveys part of "Conquest"
      included between the west line of "Bishop's Addition" and "Smith's
      Mistake" and Bishop's Cove; if in case the west line of "Bishop's
      Addition" is allowed to extend to Coursey's Point. Wits: John Haw-
      kins, R. N. Wright. Acknowledged before R. N. Wright and Thomas
      Wilkinson.

282. 10 April 1740 Richard Tilghman to John Cole - receipt for six shil-
      lings sterling, alienation on a deed recorded on folios 268, 269.

282. 26 March 1740 - 17 April 1740 Thomas Fisher, Planter, and Easter
      his wife, to John Baynard, Planter - consideration ₤69.19.0 ster-
      ling - part of "Large Range," devised by Thomas Fisher, Planter,
      26 December 1721, to his son Richard, whereon he then dwelt - Rich-
      ard is now dead without issue; Thomas, his brother is his heir at
      law. Adjoins 100 acres sold to Edward Barwick who has conveyed the
      same to John Baynard and one-third of the tract devised for life by
      Thomas Fisher, deceased, to Sarah Awsiter and after her decease to
      John Baynard. Acknowledged before R. N. Wright and Wm. Ratcliffe.
      Alienation fine, five shillings sterling.

285. 16 April 1740 - 9 May 1740 Walter Smith of St. Leonards in Calvert County, Province of Maryland, Gentleman, to Joseph Sudler, Merchant - consideration ₺200 sterling - 800 acres called "Sledmar," also known by the names of "Rousby's" and lying on the east side of Rousby's Branch. Wits: John Manning, _____ Mackgill, Walter Smith, Jr. Acknowledged before Robert Gordon by Walter Smith and Alathea, his wife. Alienation fine, ₺1.12.0 sterling.

286. 6 May 1740 - 22 May 1740 Michael Hussey, Planter, and Margarett his wife, to George Baynard, Planter - consideration 7,500 pounds of tobacco - land willed by Michael Hussey, deceased, to Michael Hussey, 18 April 1733. A plantation on the west-northwest side of a path or road that went by his plantation side from the plantation that Nicholas Sheerlock bought of Charles Lemar, Sr., to Robert Jarman, Sr.'s - reserving for his wife Catherine Hussey one-half of the plantation and one-half of the orchard for life. Michael and Margarett acknowledged before R. N. Wright and William Ratcliffe.

288. 24 June 1740 William Horney of Talbot County, Planter, and Elizabeth his wife, to James Roberts, Planter - in consideration of ye sum of half a pistole, half a crown sterling and 4,000 pounds of tobacco - 100 acres called "Dixon's Gift," on the west side of Unicorn Branch above Wilmore's Fork. Wits: William Ratcliffe, John Earle, before whom the deed was acknowledged. Alienation fine, four shillings sterling, paid to Richard Tilghman.

290. 25 June 1740 Peter Rich, Innholder, and Susanna his wife, to William Andrew, Bricklayer - consideration ₺7 sterling - 15 acres on Choptank River, part of "Ingram's Desier." Peter and Susanna acknowledged before William Ratcliffe and Joseph Sudler (she being first privately examined out of his hearing). Alienation fine, seven pence, half penny sterling.

291. 21 June 1740 - 25 June 1740 Peter Rich and Susanna his wife, to their son-in-law William Andrew, Bricklayer, and Elizabeth his wife - a gift of love for life and to their heirs forever - 100 acres, part of "Ingram's Desier," near Choptank Bridge. Alienation fine, four shillings sterling.

292. 25 June 1740 Richard Harrington, Planter, to John Colbreath, Planter - consideration ₺14 paper currency - 35 acres, part of "Solomon's Lott Addition," west side of Choptank River. Acknowledged before James Brown and Joseph Sudler. Alienation fine, one shilling, five pence sterling.

293. 26 June 1740 Thomas Hynson Wright, Gentleman, and Mary his wife, to Thomas Peacock Betts, Planter - consideration 9,600 pounds of tobacco - 100 acres of land, part of "Providence." Acknowledged before Robert Norrest Wright and Charles Downes (the said Mary being first privately examined). Alienation fine, four shillings sterling.

294. 27 June 1740 Archibald Greenfield, Mariner, to Isbel Bath, Widow –
a gift of goodwill for life – Lot Number Thirty-five with a house,
in Ogletown. Acknowledged before Thomas Wilkinson and James Brown.

295. 3 June 1740 – 1 July 1740 John Nevill, Planter, and Anne his wife,
to Josiah Coleman – consideration Ƀ100 current – a lot adjoining
Lot Number Eleven in Kings Town – on Chester River. Acknowledged
before William Ratcliffe and James Brown.

296. 29 July 1740 George Buck of Bideford, County of Devon (Eng.), Merchant, to Mr. Matthew Marsh – Letter of Attorney, dated 17 March
1739; witnessed by John Lorain and Thomas Floyd. John Lorain confirmed in the Queen Ann's County court before Thomas Hynson Wright
and Charles Downes – Thomas Floyd is runaway.

297. 29 July 1740 George Buck of Bideford, County of Devon (Eng.), to
Capt. John Martin, Commander of the ship "Globe" – Letter of Attor-
ney empowering him to settle accounts, 17 March 1739. Wits: Matt.
Marsh, John Lorain. Matthais Marsh and John Lorain confirmed before
Thomas Hynson Wright and Charles Downes.

298. 24 July 1740 – 30 July 1740 John Emory, Jr. and William Dawson,
appointed by Thomas Hynson Wright to view and value 290 acres, part
of two tracts called "Long Neck" and "Coursey Upon Wye" and the
plantation, if any, and improvements thereon; the right of Elizabeth
Turbutt, a minor under the care of Nathan Wright, guardian – find
there is no plantation or improvements thereon except about two
acres of cleared ground and about 600 old railes not of any value.

298. 27 August 1740 John Atkinson, Planter, to Benjamin Denny – consideration 12,500 pounds of tobacco – 100 acres called "Wooters Choice."
John and Joan his wife acknowledged before Thomas Wilkinson and
James Brown (the said Joan being first privately examined). Alienation fine, four shillings sterling paid to Richard Tilghman.

300. 26 August 1740 – 27 August 1740 William Bishop, Gentleman, to Thomas Hynson Wright – consideration 19,300 pounds of tobacco and Ƀ12
sterling – 200 acres in Spanyards Neck, part of "Coursey's Point,"
now "Smith's Mistake." Acknowledged before William Ratcliffe and
Thomas Wilkinson. Alienation fine, four pence, half penny sterling.

302. 16 August 1740 – 27 August 1740 William Wilkerson, Jr. and Adam
Wilkerson, Planters, to John Comergys – consideration 2,000 pounds
of tobacco – 200 acres called "Shepard's Redoubt" – execpting 100
acres already sold to James Roberts – lying on Red Lyon Branch and
adjoining the land of Thomas Collins; and "Slarterton;" the remaining part, 200 acres. William, Adam and Mary wife of Adam Wilkerson,
acknowledged before James Brown and John Earle (Mary being first
privately examined).

303. 26 August 1740 – 28 August 1740 Thomas Hussey and Rachel his wife,
to Baldwin Kemp – consideration 8,000 pounds of tobacco and Ƀ3 cur-

303. rent money - 91 acres of land, part of "Hinesleys Plains" in Tully's Neck - adjoining "Allcock's Pharsalia." Thomas and Rachel (she being first privately examined) acknowledged their deed before William Ratcliffe and James Brown.

305. 1 August 1740 - 28 August 1740 Thomas Hynson Wright to William Kent, Planter - consideration 2,500 pounds of tobacco - 50 acres, part of "Tom's Fancy Enlarged," adjoining the part where Kent now dwells - an oversight made in a deed dated 18 November 1738 of part of the same tract. Wits: T. Wilkinson, John Downes, Jr. Acknowledged before Charles Downes and Thomas Wilkinson. Alienation fine, two shillings sterling, paid to Richard Tilghman.

306. 28 August 1740 Thomas Vanderford, Planter, to William Clayton, William Clayton, Jr. and William Coursey, Gentlemen, executors of Solomon Clayton, deceased - consideration 5,820 pounds of tobacco - 90 acres, part of "Fox Hill," and 37 acres, part of "Notley's Delight" - a mortgage due with interest by 10 March next. Acknowledged before Thomas Wilkinson and William Ratcliffe.

307. 26 April 1740 - 30 August 1740 John Earle and Ernault Hawkins, appointed by Robert Norrest Wright to view and value 100 acres of land called "Alder Branch" and the plantation and improvements thereon, the right of Michael Green, a minor; under the care of Thomas Meridith, guardian - find about 12 apple trees and the fencing very much out of repair - we find no houses on the plantation. The rent, Ŀ40 yearly - the guardian allowed to clear 20 acres.

307. 26 August 1740 - 11 September 1740 William Bishop and Anne his wife, to William Vanderford - consideration 6,000 pounds of tobacco - part of "Fox Hill," 85 acres lying on Hambleton's Branch. William and Anne (she being first privately examined) acknowledged before James Brown and William Ratcliffe. Alienation fine, three shillings, five pence, paid to Richard Tilghman.

309. 25 August 1740 - 15 September 1740 John Hawkins, Jr. to Edward Brown - one negro boy named "Georg," about sixteen years of age.

309. NOTICE. The ship "Crichton" of London, William Anderson, Commander, lying in Chester River, takes in tobacco consigned to James Buchanan, Merchant, at Ŀ9 sterling per tonn. September 12, 1740.

309. 21 April 1740 - 27 September 1740 John Hawkins, Gentleman, to Bedingfield Hands of Kent County, Merchant - in consideration of the rents and further payment of five shillings sterling - leases 175 acres called "Tully's Delight" and a parcel of plantable land, part of "Macklinborough," from 1 April for a term of one year. Wits: John Gresham, Thomas Gough. Recorded in the Provincial Office - W. Ghisolm, Clerk.

310. 22 April 1740 - 22 September 1740 An indenture tripartite between

310. John Hawkins, Bedingfield Hands of Kent County, Merchant, and James
Smith, Gentleman, of Kent County - to dock and bar the above lands -
involves a writ of entry . Wits: Henry Hooper, Joshua George.
Alienation fine of twenty shillings for "Tully's Delight" and six
shillings for part of "Macklinborough, paid to Benjamin Tasker,
8 May 1740.

312. 5 November 1740 William Elice of Kent County, Carpenter, to William
Barkhurst, Planter - consideration 3,000 pounds of tobacco - 50
acres, a tract of land called "Pensilvania Border" - lying on the
east side of Chester River - below an old poplar tree being the
southwest corner tree of Governour Penn's Mannor of Pensilvania.
Sig: William Ellis. Acknowledged before William Ratcliffe and James
Brown. Alienation fine, two shillings sterling, paid to Richard
Tilghman.

313. 19 August 1740 - 17 November 1740 Samuel Ratcliff of Talbot County,
Planter, to James Ratcliff of Talbot County - consideration 1,333
pounds of tobacco and ₤6.13.4 current whole gold of the Province
and ₤13.6.6 current paper money of the Province - 100 acres, part of
"Jerusalem," on the Southeast Branch of Chester River. Wits: Thomas
Bullen, W. Thomas. Robert Harwood and Edmond Farrell witnessed the
receipt Samuel gave to James, 19 August 1740. Samuel acknowledged
before Thomas Bullen and William Thomas, Justices of the Peace for
Talbot County - certified by John Leeds, Clerk. Alienation fine,
four shillings sterling, paid to Richard Tilghman.

315. 11 April 1740 - 20 November 1740 Charles Calvert, Lord Proprietory
of the Province, to Edward Tilghman, Gentleman - appointment to be
Receiver, Bailiff and Collector of quitrents and reserved rents in
the county of Queen Anne. per Samuel Ogle, Governor.

315. 22 November 1740 - 27 November 1740 Morgin Ponder, Planter, to John
Collins - consideration ₤30 current - 50 acres, part of "Poplar
Hill," on the south side of Chester River. Acknowledged before
William Ratcliffe and James Brown. Alienation fine, two shillings
sterling.

317. 28 November 1740 Thomas Hynson Wright, Gentleman, and Mary his wife
to John Atkinson, Planter - consideration 24,000 pounds of tobacco -
200 acres in Tully's Neck, part of "Tom's Fancy Enlarged." Acknowledged before Thomas Wilkinson and James Brown (Mary being first
privately examined). Alienation fine, eight shillings sterling.

318. 28 November 1740 - 1 December 1740 John Harding, Planter, to Frances Elbert, Widow - consideration 5,000 pounds of tobacco - a negro
woman named "Phyllis." Wits: Robert Lloyd, James Tilghman. Acknowledged before Robert Lloyd.

319. NOTICE. Richard Flood, Commander of the Snow, "Prince of Orange,"
now riding at anchor in Wye River, bound to London, will take tobac-

319. co on board his Snow at ₤9 sterling per tonn, consigned to James Buchanan, Merchant. 10 November 1740.

319. 15 January 1740 - 22 January 1740 Henry Bennett to John Hackett - consideration ₤60 current - a negro slave called "Ben." Acknowledged before Arthur Holt and James Brown.

320. 16 August 1740 - 11 February 1740 Moris Cloak of Kent County, Maryland, Planter, to Jonathon Jolley of Queen Ann's County - consideration 1,500 pounds of tobacco - 50 acres, part of "Andover," on Andover Branch. Acknowledged before John Earle and Humphery Wells, Jr. Alienation fine, two shillings sterling, paid to Richard Tilghman. Sig: Moris Cloke.

321. 16 April 1740 - 11 February 1740 John Nicholson of Kent County, Planter, to Jonathon Jolley - consideration 1,300 pounds of tobacco - 50 acres called "Nicholson's Venture," lying between Andover and Unicorn Branches. Acknowledged before John Earle and Humphery Wells, Jr. Alienation fine, two shillings sterling.

323. 19 February 1740 - 23 February 1740 Elizabeth Hawkins, Widow, to John Gibb, Gentleman - consideration 9,000 pounds of tobacco - 244 acres, part of "Knowles' Range" - on the south side of the Unicorn Branch - adjoining "Robotham's Park." Acknowledged before Thomas Wilkinson and Robert Lloyd. Alienation fine, nine shillings, nine pence, half penny sterling.

324. 25 February 1740 Thomas Hynson Wright to John Deford and Anne his wife - in consideration of 70 acres, part of "Lowe's Arcadia" - conveyed 91 acres in Tully's Neck, part of "Tom's Fancy Enlarged." Acknowledged before R. N. Wright and Robert Lloyd.

325. 26 February 1740 Thomas Hynson Wright to his nephew, Hynson Wright - in consideration of natural love and affection - 100 acres of land, part of "Tom's Fancy Enlarged," adjoining the east side of Chester Marsh. Acknowledged before Thomas Wilkinson and R. Lloyd.

326. NOTICE. The ship "Mary," Thomas Reed, Master, lying in Wye River and bound for London, takes in freight consigned to James Buchanan at ₤10 sterling per tonn. Maryland, March 7, 1740.

326. 28 February 1740 - 12 March 1740 William Bishop, Gentleman, and Anne his wife, to Thomas Butler, Planter - consideration 5,000 pounds of tobacco and ₤8 currency - 85 acres, part of "Fox Hill" - west side of Hambleton's Branch. William and Anne (she being first privately examined) acknowledged before Robert Norrest Wright and Thomas Wilkinson. Alienation fine, three shillings, five pence sterling paid to Richard Tilghman.

327. 26 January 1740 - 12 March 1740 Thomas Vanderford, Planter, and Rosanna his wife, to Thomas Butler, Planter - consideration 3,000 pounds of tobacco - 37 acres, part of "Notlar's Delight" - lying

327. on the south side of Hambleton's Branch - adjoining "Fox Hill" and
a part sold by Nicholas Clouds to Henry Johnson. Thomas and Rosanna
(she being first privately examined) acknowledged before James Brown
and John Earle. Alienation fine, one shilling, six pence paid to
Richard Tilghman.

328. 21 February 1749 - 12 March 1740 George Gale and John Gale of Som-
erset County in Maryland, Gentlemen, to James Bartlett of Talbot
County, Carpenter - consideration ₤80 current - 575 acres of land
called "Partnership" - patented 2 November 1738 by George and John
Gale. Wits: James Johnson, Matthais Gale. Acknowledged before Levin
Gale, Justice of the Provincial Court.

329. 12 March 1740 Christopher Cox and Margerett his wife, to their children - in consideration of love, goodwill and affection - to their
son James Cox, a negro boy named "Anthony" als "Tony;" to their
daughter Anne Cox, a negro girl named "Susanna" als "Sue;" to their
daughter Martha Cox, a negro girl name "Minte:" to their son Christopher Cox, Jr., a tract of land called "Plaindealing," devised to
Margaret Cox by her father, James Earle - formerly lying in Talbot
County but now in Queen Ann's County, west side of Broadrib's Branch
of Island Creek - bounded according to patent. Christopher and Margaret (she being first privately examined) acknowledged their deed of
gift before Thomas Hynson Wright and Charles Downes. Sig: Margaret
Cox.

330. 16 March 1740 - 24 March 1740 Thomas Wilkinson, Gentleman, and
Elizabeth his wife, to James Cox, Gentleman - consideration 2,900
pounds of tobacco - 29 acres, all of "Doctor's Folly," lying on the
south side of the main road westward and adjoining Saint Paul's
Church and churchyard; and "Denby," now in Cox's possession. Acknowledged before T. H. Wright and C. Downes. Alienation fine, one
shilling, two pence, half penny sterling.

333. 25 November 1740 - 24 March 1740 David Pritchard of Talbot County,
Cordwinder, and Mary his wife, to Samuel Field, Planter - consideration 3,000 pounds of tobacco - 100 acres, part of "Benjamin's In-
fancy" - lying on the south side of the Frenchwoman's Branch of Tuckahoe Creek - adjoining the lands of Thomas Porter and "Suffolk."
David and Mary (she being first privately examined) acknowledged before Robert Lloyd and William Ratcliffe. Alienation fine, four shillings sterling, paid to Richard Tilghman.

335. 25 March 1741 Charles Loud, Planter, to George Robins, Gentleman -
consideration ₤40 current - 105 acres, being one-half of "Sylvester's Forrest," in Tuckahoe Neck; also 90 acres adjoining, one-half
of "Cary's Discovery." Acknowledged before Robert Lloyd and James
Brown.

337. 25 March 1741 Thomas Baily, Sr. to his son Thomas Baily, Jr. - gift
of love - 100 acres, part of "Bradbourne's Delight," lying on a cove

337. of Courseygale Creek. Acknowledged before Robert Norrest Wright
and Thomas Wilkinson.

337. 25 March 1741 Richard Tilghman to James Bartlett - receipt of one
pound, three shillings sterling, alienation fine for the deed recorded on folios 328 and 329.

338. 26 March 1741 Joseph Hunter and Mary his wife, to Lawrance Everet
of Kent Island - consideration ₤20 current - 100 acres, part of
"Hunter's Forrest" - lying on the east side of Tuckahoe Creek. Joseph and Mary (she being first privately examined) acknowledged before Joseph Sudler and John Earle. Alienation fine, four shillings
sterling.

339. 23 February 1740 - 27 March 1741 John Hackett and Thomas Hackett,
appointed by John Earle to view and value 200 acres of land, part of
"Gold's Purchase" and the plantation and improvements thereon - the
right of James Gould, a minor, Richard Gold his guardian - find one
old dwelling house, 32 feet long in ordinary repair; one old kitchen
ready to fall down; one old cornhouse, 20 feet long; three old houses, 10 feet long each in ordinary repair; ten old apple trees,
three pare trees; the fencing in ordinary repair; one brick oven.

340. 27 February 1740 - 30 March 1741 Thomas Hynson Wright, Gentleman,
to James Earle - consideration 7,000 pounds of tobacco - 162 acres,
part of "Tom's Fancy Enlarged" - adjoining John Atkinson's part.
Acknowledged before Charles Downes and Thomas Wilkinson.

341. 3 April 1741 Francis Barnes to Thomas Barnes - consideration 2,500
pounds of tobacco - all rights to 323 acres of land called "Barnes'
Satisfaction" - lying on Kent Island. Francis Barnes and Jane his
wife (she being first privately examined) acknowledged before William Jumpe and Thomas Wilkinson.

342. 10 April 1741 - 23 April 1741 John Dempster, Planter, to Thomas
Lihon(?) of the Island of Garnsey, now residing at Chester Town,
Mariner - consideration ₤10 current - Lott Number Three in Kings
Town. Acknowledged before John Earle and James Brown.

343. 7 May 1741 Richard Tilghman to Thomas Baily, Jr. - receipt of four
shillings sterling, alienation fine for deed recorded folio 337.

343. 1 May 1741 - 30 May 1741 Thomas Hynson Wright to John Downes, Planter - in consideration of certain services done - 160 acres of land,
part of "Wright's Reserve," lying in the Long Neck. Acknowledged
before Charles Downes and Thomas Wilkinson. Alienation fine, six
shillings, five pence sterling.

344. 25 February 1740 - 11 June 1741 John Deford and Anne his wife, formerly called Anne Tomlin, to Thomas Hynson Wright - in consideration
of 90 acres, part of "Tom's Fancy Enlarged" - conveys 70 acres of
land, part of "Lowe's Arcadia," heretofore conveyed from Joan Taylor,

344. Widow, to her grandchild Anne Tomlin, now Anne Deford, 27 June 1716, adjoining part given by his mother to Samuel Taylor. John and Anne (she being first privately examined) acknowledged before Robert N. Wright and Robert Lloyd. Alienation fine, two shillings, ten pence sterling, paid to Richard Tilghman.

345. 8 February 1740 - 17 June 1741 Robert Knatchbull, Gentleman, now residing at Liege in parts beyond the seas, to Richard Bennett of Wye River, Esquire - consideration five shillings - one-year lease of 270 acres, part of "Young's Chance;" also 132 acres, part of "Lambeth Fields." Wits: Henry Neale, Richard Archibold.

346. 9 February 1740 - 17 June 1741 Robert Knatchbull, Richard Bennett and James Tuit and Mary his wife, a sister to Robert Knatchbull - a deed tripartite - in consideration of love for his sister and her children and ten shillings paid by Bennett - conveyed the above land to Bennett, in trust for his sister during her lifetime and after her death to her sons according to seniority; and without such to her female children. 12 March 1740 Henry Neale confirmed the deed before Thomas Wilkinson and Robert Lloyd.

348. 15 June 1741 - 18 June 1741 Nathan Richardson of Baltimore County and Elizabeth his wife, to Thomas Price, son of William Price, deceased - consideration ₤60 current money - 100 acres, part of "Clover Field," bequeathed to Nathan Richardson by Benjamin Ball, late of Kent Island and originally possessed by William Dawkins. Wits: Levin Gale, John Gale, Joseph Hill. 15 June 1741 Acknowledged before Levin Gale.

350. 23 June 1741 Jacob Boon, Planter, to Joseph Hunter, Planter - consideration ₤14.8.0 - 50 acres, all of "Boon's Ridge," lying in the Forrest of Choptank on the White Tree Branch. Acknowledged before William Jumpe and R. N. Wright. Alienation fine, two shillings.

351. 21 April 1741 Edward Cockey and Robert Small, appointed by Joseph Sudler to view and value the plantation of Valentine Carter, John Elliott, Sr., his guardian - find one 25 foot dwelling house, rough work; one 40 foot tobacco house; one 30 foot tobacco house, both rough work, the said houses in tolerable repair. Since there is not much ground cleared, the guardian is permitted to clear any that is necessary. Rent, 400 pounds of tobacco per annum.

351. 21 April 1741 Edward Cockey and Robert Small, appointed by Joseph Sudler, to view and value the plantation of Henry Carter, Jacob Carter, his guardian - find one 24 foot dwelling house with an 8 foot shed at one end, in tolerable repair; one 40 foot tobacco house, rough work, in tolerable repair; one 30 foot ditto, old and out of repair; eight old apple trees; a 16 foot cornhouse out of repair; 1,105 pannells of fencing; Jacob to clear only for tobacco beds. Rent, 450 pounds of tobacco per annum.

351. 15 July 1741 - 22 July 1741 Thomas Hynson Wright to William Docwra - consideration 11,520 pounds of tobacco - 192 acres, part of
"Moor's Hope Addition" - beginning at the original tree of "Mist
Hit," formerly surveyed for Stephen Rich - lying on the Chester
Mill Branch of Corsica Creek. Thomas Hynson Wright to William Docwra - receipt for 11,520 pounds of tobacco, by the hand of Matthew
Docwra. Acknowledged before Robert Norrest Wright and Thomas Wilkinson. Alienation fine paid to R. Tilghman, seven shillings,
eight pence sterling.

354. 15 July 1741 - 22 July 1741 Thomas Hynson Wright to Matthew Docwra - consideration 6,000 pounds of tobacco - 100 acres, all of
"Moore's Hope," lying on the west side of Chester Mill Branch about
one mile above Stephen Rich's plantation. Alienation fine, four
shillings sterling.

356. 15 July 1741 - 22 July 1741 Thomas Hynson Wright to Matthew Doc-
wra - consideration 12,480 pounds of tobacco - 208 acres, part of
"Moore's Hope Addition." Acknowledged before R. N. Wright and
Thomas Wilkinson. Alienation fine, eight shillings, four pence.

358. 17 July 1741 - 22 July 1741 William Dockery, the son, and Mary
Dockery (widow and relict of Matthais Dockery) to Matthew Dockery -
(son of Matthais Dockery) - in consideration of 100 acres, part of
"Moore's Hope Addition" with one dwelling house and tobacco house
thereon, to the liking of him, the said William, purchased by the
said Matthew, the son, from Thomas Hynson Wright, 15 July inst. -
conveys a quit claim to part of "Fishingham," with the plantation
thereon, devised by Matthais Dockery, 15 December 1740, to his son,
William - his dwelling plantation with fifty acres of land, part of
"Fishingham;" after the death of his wife Mary Dockery, but if his
son Matthew should purchase for William 100 acres of land to his
liking with a dwelling house and tobacco house, then he gave his
dwelling plantation to his son, Matthew. William and Mary acknowledged their deed before Thomas H. Wright and Charles Downes (the
said Mary being first privately examined). Alienation fine, two
shillings sterling.

359. 27 February 1740 - 23 July 1741 Thomas Hynson Wright to Charles
Lizenby, Planter - in consideration of some services done by John
Lizenby, father of Charles - conveys 50 acres, part of "Tom's Fan-
cy Enlarged" in Tully's Neck, adjoining a tract sold to John Lloyd
and Nathaniel Read. Acknowledged before Charles Downes and Thomas
Wilkinson.

360. 23 July 1741 Richard Tilghman to James Tuit - receipt for eleven
shillings two pence sterling, alienation fine for folios 346, 347
and 348.

360. 27 July 1741 - 30 July 1741 Alice Collier, Widow, to Thomas Hynson
Wright - a deed of release on part of two tracts called "Bishop's
Outlet" and "Bishop's Addition," containing 300 acres. The land

360. was purchased by Alice Collier as Alice Austin, which afterwards became possessed by Matthew Collier who by a codicil to his will
devised the same to Alice. The metes and bounds are now uncertain
and T. H. Wright hath of late purchased of William Bishop all of the
remainder of the two tracts and this release given in order to settle any differences arising concerning their respective claims.
Acknowledged before Robert Norrest Wright and Thomas Wilkinson.

361. 22 June 1741 - 6 August 1741 John Dempster to Henry Cully of Chester Town in Kent County, Province of Maryland, Merchant - consideration ₤30 current - Lott Number One in Kings Town in Queen Ann's
County, called the Prize House Lott and also a piece of land lying
between that lott and Chester River. John Dempster and Joan his
wife (she being first privately examined) acknowledged before James
Brown and John Earle.

362. 6 August 1741 John Dempster leases to Henry Cully of Chester Town,
Kent County, Merchant, 12 acres of land adjoining Kings Town in
Queen Ann's County - part of "Poplar Hill." Adjoining Lott Number
One and running along the river to intersect Fishing Creek - for and
during the life of Henry Cully and the natural life of Christian,
wife of Henry Cully, and the life of David Dempster, son of John,
the yearly rent, ten shillings current money. 22 June 1741. Acknowledged before James Brown and John Earle.

363. 7 July 1741 - 6 August 1741 Thomas Roe, Planter, to Joseph Merchant - consideration 1,500 pounds of tobacco - 50 acres called
"Musketo Ridge," lying in ye Forrest of Choptank on the south side
of the Cross Marsh. Acknowledged before Robert N. Wright and James
Brown. Alienation fine, two shillings sterling.

364. 6 August 1741 Richard Tilghman to Charles Lizenby - receipt for two
shillings sterling, alienation fine for folios 359 and 360.

364. 10 August 1741 - 22 August 1741 Christopher Burch to William Giles
of Bideford, Mariner, Factor for Samuel Banbury & Company - consideration ₤12 current and 1,095 pounds of tobacco - a servant man
named William Trevillian, a convict under transportation for seven
years. Wits: William Hopper, Joseph Burch. Acknowledged before
Thomas Hynson Wright.

365. 25 August 1741 - 26 August 1741 Henry Jacobs, Planter, and Anne his
wife, to Thomas McClannahane, Planter - in consideration of 11,600
pounds of tobacco - part of "Fox Harbour," lying in a fork of Hambleton's Branch, above where Richard Clouds did dwell, 100 acres; also
56 acres on south side of Hambleton's Branch, part of "Collins Lott;"
also 42½ acres, part of "Brotherhood," on the south side of Hambleton's Branch - adjoining "Barton" and "Notlar's Desire." Henry and
Anne (she being first privately examined) acknowledged before William Jumpe and James Brown.

366. 28 August 1741 Richard Tilghman to John Deford - receipt for three

366. shillings, eight pence, alienation fine for folios 324 and 325.

367. 17 April 1741   Edward Brown and Nathan Wright, appointed by Robert
Norrest WRight to estimate the yearly value of 200 acres, part of
"Chesterfield" and 70 acres called "Chesterfield Addition," and 200
acres, part of "Neglect," and another tract called "Clayton's Levells," containing 100 acres, with the plantations and improvements
thereon, the right of Edward Clayton, a minor, Mary Clayton his
guardian - find on "Chesterfield" and "Chesterfield Addition," one
dwelling, part old, part new, 55 feet long, 16 feet wide, with a
12 foot shed, the old part much out of repair; a milk house, part
brick and part clapboards, 26 x 15 feet, in good repair; a clapboard
kitchen with a shed and a stack of brick chimneys, 40 x 20 feet,
very old and much decayed; a storehouse with sheds at each end,
25 x 16 feet, much out of repair; a log'd quarter with a brick chimney, 20 x 15 feet; a log'd corn house, 15 x 8 feet in good repair.
A tobacco house, bastard framed, 40 x 20 feet in good repair; two
log'd houses, each 20 x 16 feet, very old and much decayed; smith's
shop, 15 feet square, very old and decayed and an old tan house; a
small, young apple orchard about 60 trees; ground paled in for a
garden, 100 x 75 feet; the fencing tolerable good. The yearly value
estimated at 1,400 pounds of tobacco clear of quitrents and necessary repairs. On "Neglect" an old clapboard dwelling house with
wood chimney, 15 feet square; a cornhouse, 16 x 8 feet in good repair; tobacco house, bastard framed, 52 x 22 feet, the cover will
soon want repairing; the fencing tolerable good. Yearly value, 500
pounds of tobacco clear of quitrents, etc. The guardian is not permitted to clear any more land or to cut down any timber except for
tobacco hogsheads; necessary repairs; tobacco beds and firewood.
"Clayton's Levells" is without any plantation or improvements and
not of any annual value; the guardian is permitted to clear 40 acres
and cut necessary timber for building.

368. 27 April 1741 - 2 September 1741   John Carpenter, Planter, to Edward Tilghman, Gentleman - in consideration of ₤120 paper currency -
300 acres called "Porter's Lodge," purchased by John Carpenter, his
father, from Mordecai Hammond of Ann Arrundell County and Frances,
his wife. Refers to a mortgage of ₤60 paper money against "Porter's
Lodge," made 18 July 1735, given to Commissioners and Trustees for
Emitting Bills of Credit. Wits: Samuel Chew, Samuel Johns. John
Carpenter appointed Daniel Newnam, Jr., his attorney to acknowledge
the deed, 19 August; Samuel Johns, a Quaker, witnessed the Power of
Attorney and so acknowledged to Samuel Chamberlaine. Newnam acknowledged the deed before Robert Lloyd and John Earle. Alienation
fine, twelve shillings sterling, paid to Richard Tilghman.

370. 28 April 1741 - 2 September 1741   William Carpenter of New Castle
County on Delaware, to Edward Tilghman - consideration five shill-
ings - a quit claim to "Porter's Lodge." 20 April 1741   William
Carpenter of Kent County on Delaware, to John Emory, Jr. - Power of
Attorney to acknowledge the release.

23.

371. 2 September 1741 - 1 October 1741 Richard Bennett, Merchant, to
Charles Price, Planter - consideration 11,000 pounds of tobacco -
247 acres, part of "Broomely Lambeth" - lying between the heads of
the branches of Wye River and Corsica Creek - adjoining "Lincolne,"
now in the possession of Charles Price, near the head of Williams'
Branch. Wits: Thomas Clarke, John Loockerman, Jr. Acknowledged
before Levin Gale, a Justice of the Provincial Court. Alienation
fine, nine shillings, eleven pence sterling, paid to R. Tilghman.

372. 3 October 1741 - 12 October 1741 Morgan Ponder, Planter, to Samuel
Massey of Kent County, Province of Maryland, Hatter - consideration
£63 current money - 50 acres of land, furthest from the river, part
of 100 acres of "Poplar Hill," conveyed by William Eubanks to Ponder 9 June 1724 - 50 acres of which hath lately been sold to John
Collins and since vested in Henry Rippon, lately deceased. Acknowledged before James Brown and John Earle. Alienation fine, two
shillings sterling.

374. 18 May 1741 - 12 October 1741 Jane Thomas of Talbot County, Widow,
to her son William Thomas - a gift of love - 135 acres called "Hampton" - lying in Queen Ann's County on Williams' Branch and bound on
the southwest by Elliott's Branch - adjoining a parcel of land formerly laid out for Robert Smith, late in the possession of Daniel
Demsley. Also 100 acres, "Smith's Range." Acknowledged in Talbot
County court before Thomas Bozman and Thomas Bullen. Certified by
John Leeds, Clerk of Talbot County.

376. 5 November 1741 Thomas Wilkinson, Gentleman, to the Reverend Mr.
James Cox, Robert Lloyd, William Hopper, John Brown, Arthur Emory,
Jr., Christopher Cox and Richard Tilghman, Vestry Men of St. Paul's
Parish - consideration five shillings - one-half acre, part of a
tract called "Doctor's Folly" - adjoining a part lately sold to Reverend James Cox. Acknowledged before Thomas Hynson Wright and Robert Norrest Wright.

377. 27 October 1741 - 5 November 1741 Mary Clayton, Widow, to her niece,
Sarah Coursey, daughter of William Coursey - a gift of love - one
mulatto girl called "Doll," about four years of age. Wits: Thomas
Lane, Sarah Wright.

377. 12 November 1741 Thomas Price, son of William Price, from Richard
Tilghman - receipt of four shillings sterling, alienation fine for
folios 348 and 349.

377. 19 November 1741 Thomas Hinesly, Planter, to James Barwick, Planter - consideration 2,000 pounds of tobacco - 60 acres, part of
"Oaken Thorp," lying in Tully's Neck on the Beaver Dam Branch. Wits:
James Earle, Ambrose Wright. Acknowledged before Thomas Wilkinson
and John Earle. Alienation fine two shillings, five pence sterling.

379. 19 November 1741 - 20 November 1741 James Kersey, Sr., Planter, to
Thomas Kersey, Planter - consideration 2,000 pounds of tobacco -

379. 50 acres, part of "Shetland," on Brodrib's Branch - adjoining "Good Increase," which Thomas Cruper doth now hold. Acknowledged before Thomas Wilkinson and John Earle.

380. 19 November 1741 - 20 November 1741 James Kersey, Sr., Planter, to William Carman, Planter - consideration 2,000 pounds of tobacco - 50 acres on Broadrib's Branch, part of "Shetland." Receipt for two shillings sterling, alienation fine, given to Thomas Kersey.

381. 18 November 1741 - 20 November 1741 Alexander King, Weaver, to his wife Mary King - (except for one featherbed and furniture) all of his goods, chattels and substance. Wits: Thomas Wilkinson, George Mattershaw, Thomas Clarke.

381. 20 November 1741 Mary King, wife of Alexander King, having received his deed of gift for all of his personal estate (except one featherbed and furniture), the said deed of gift is annexed as remaining to me after his decease and not otherwise. 18 November 1741.

382. 22 June 1741 - 25 November 1741 William Ginniss, Mariner, to Lambert Wilmer of Kent County, Province of Maryland, Gentleman - consideration ₤11 current money - Lott Number Fifteen in Kings Town, purchased of John Dempster. Acknowledged before James Brown and James Earle. Sig: William Gennys.

383. 25 November 1741 Richard Tilghman to Henry Cully - receipt of three farthings sterling, alienation fine for folios 361 and 362.

383. 12 November 1741 - 26 November 1741 William Bishop to Thomas Seward - consideration 20,000 pounds of tobacco - 174 acres of land in the fork of Hambleton's Branch called "Outrange." Acknowledged before James Brown and John Earle. Alienation fine, seven shillings sterling.

384. 10 November 1741 - 26 November 1741 Francis Spry, Jr., Planter, and Elizabeth his wife, daughter and devisee of John Hacket, to James Brown, Gentleman - one-third of 100 acres on Hambleton's Branch, part of "Hambleton's Hermitage," purchased by John Hacket of William Hambleton of Talbot County and his wife Margrett, 12 February 1701. Devised by Hackett to his three daughters, Rachell, Hannah and Elizabeth Hackett, to be equally divided. The consideration, 900 pounds of tobacco, paid by Brown. Acknowledged before Thomas Hynson Wright and Humphery Wells, Jr. (Elizabeth having first been privately examined). Alienation fine, eight shillings sterling paid to Richard Tilghman.

386. 27 November 1741 - 28 November 1741 James Millis, Planter, and Jane his wife, to Richard Harrington, Planter - consideration 3,000 pounds of tobacco - 50 acres, one-half of "Fisher's Chance" - on Choptank River. Wits: William Goldsborough, James Tilghman. Acknowledged at court in Queenstown before Thomas Hynson Wright and Associate Justices. Test: Richard Tilghman, Clerk.

25.

387. 21 September 1741 - 30 November 1741 Matthew Read and Henrietta
his wife, eldest son and heir at law of Matthew Read, deceased; eldest son and devisee of Matthew Read the elder, deceased, to Thomas
Hynson Wright - WHEREAS, Matthew Read the elder, died possessed of
"Reading," formerly granted to him for 450 acres and by his will devised to his son Matthew Read and his heirs forever, who afterwards
died and devised the same to his two sons Matthew and Nathaniel,
equally - which said Matthew and Nathaniel upon inspection into the
premises found the tract according to the courses thereof, did include a considerable quantity of navigable water and therefore did
obtain a special warrant to resurvey the same with liberty to ex-
clude the water, which was accordingly resurveyed and called "New
Reading;" and afterwards Matthew and Nathaniel sold to Thomas Hynson Wright several parcels of the said tract and after that Matthew
Read died before the pattent of confirmation did issue which hath
since been granted to Nathaniel and Matthew Read, party to these
presents as heirs at law to Matthew Read, devisee as above. In consideration of 100 acres of land, part of "Gray's Inn," made over to
Matthew Read by Thomas Hynson Wright this date and ₤75 sterling,
Read conveyed 1,200 acres, part of "New Reading" whereon the said
Matthew Read now dwells. Acknowledged before Robert Norris Wright
and Charles Downes (the said Henrietta Read having first been privately examined out of hearing of her husband). Alienation fine,
two shillings, five pence sterling.

389. 25 July 1740 William Campbell and John Clayland, appointed by Thomas Hynson Wright to view and value 139¼ acres, part of "Mt. Mill"
and part of "Addition," and part of "Bennett's Outlet" with the
plantations and improvements thereon and one watermill, being the
right of John Seth, a minor, now under the care of Nathaniel Connor, his guardian - find one old dwelling house, 50 x 20 feet with
one brick gable end and chimney, very much out of repair; one old
dwelling house in the shape of an ell, the one part 30 x 17 feet
with a stack of brick chimneys in the middle, in good repair, the
other part, 25 x 15 feet in middling repair; one brick milk house
14 x 8 feet; one old meat house 11 x 10 feet, much out of repair;
one old log'd corn house 14 x 6 feet; one old hen house 10 feet
square, out of repair; one good brick oven; one framed barn 40 x 20
feet in reasonable repair; one old 30 foot tobacco house, 20 feet
wide very much out of repair; one old tobacco house 40 x 15 feet
very much out of repair; and a small old orchard belonging to the
dwelling plantation and about 100 acres of cleared ground under a
reasonable good fencing; and upon the plantation where Thomas Johnings dwells, one old dwelling house 25 x 15 feet; one small log'd
kitchen 15 x 12 feet and one old logg'd corn house, all very mean;
and about 50 acres of cleared ground under a reasonable good fencing; both which places the annual value is estimated to be 1,600
pounds of tobacco clear of quitrents and necessary repairs; one-
fourth part belongs to John Seth, the minor; with liberty of timber and 6 acres of ground to clear. We have also viewed one old
water mill which house is 20 feet square and very old and out of repair, both house and geer; the annual value 1,000 pounds of tobacco

389. clear of necessary repairs, with liberty of timber for repairs.

391. 21 September 1741 - 12 January 1741 Matthew Read and Henrietta his
wife, to Nathaniel Read - in consideration that Nathaniel Read and
Sarah his wife by a deed of division of equal date, released all of
the remaining part of "New Reading" - remise part of "New Reading"
on the Deep Branch - adjoining part sold to Thomas Hynson Wright.
Reference made to the will of Matthew Read, Sr. Acknowledged before
Robert Norrest Wright and Charles Downes.

392. 24 July 1741 - 12 January 1741 Thomas Hynson Wright to Alice Collier, Widow - division of lands called "Bishop's Addition" and "Bishop's Outlet," 300 acres purchased by Alice under the name of Alice
Austin and afterwards the possession of Matthew Collier, deceased,
who by way of a codicill to his will devised to Alice. The metes
and bounds of the lands are uncertain and as Thomas Hynson Wright
hath lately purchased of William Bishop all of the remaining part of
the two tracts, the two parties agree to divide to prevent further
dispute. In consideration of a deed of release, Wright conveys part
of the land lying on Corsica Creek (metes and bounds given) - adjoining Green's land. Acknowledged before Robert Norrest WRight and
Thomas Wilkinson.

393. 6 October 1741 - 21 January 1741 Nathaniel Knotts and Susannah his
wife, to Joseph Merchant - consideration 3,190 pounds of tobacco -
"Littleworth," 50 acres lying between Island Marsh of Tuckahoe Creek
and the Short Marsh. Wits: John Earle, Robert Norrest Wright, before
whom Nathaniel and Susannah acknowledged (she being first privately
examined). Alienation fine, two shillings sterling, paid to Richard
Tilghman.

395. 27 January 1741 Thomas Reed, Commander of the ship "Mary," lying at
anchor in Wye River and bound to London, will take on board on
freight at ₤9 sterling per tonn, consigned to James Buchanan, Merchant in London.

395. 28 February 1741 - 11 March 1741 Henry Downes, Planter, and Frances
his wife, to John Downes, Planter - consideration ₤6.7.0 - 22 acres,
part of "Carter's Forrest" - beginning at the first tree of "Noble's
Range" and adjoining John Emerson's land. Henry and Frances (she
being first privately examined) acknowledged before Thomas Wilkinson
and Robert Lloyd. Alienation fine, eleven pence sterling.

397. 24 March 1741 William Jurdan, Planter, and Elizabeth his wife, to
John Burk, Sr., Planter - consideration 1,440 pounds of tobacco -
48 acres, part of "Coldrayn," formerly laid out for John Pitt of Talbot County - on the road leading from Tully's Neck Bridge to Tuckahoe
Bridge - adjoining land conveyed by John Croney to his daughter, Margaret Burk. Wits: John Croney, John Burk, Jr. William and Elizabeth
(she being first privately examined) acknowledged before Thomas Hynson Wright and Associates. Richard Tilghman, Clerk of Court. Alienation fine, eleven pence, half penny sterling.

398. 26 February 1741 - 11 March 1741 Edward Harden of Talbot County, Planter, and Rose his wife, to John Downes - consideration 4,500 pounds of tobacco - 75 acres, part of "Hemsley's Arcadia" - adjoining "Noble's Range." Edward and Rose (she being first privately examined) acknowledged before Thomas Wilkinson and Robert Lloyd. Alienation fine, three shillings sterling, paid to Richard Tilghman.

400. 1 March 1741 - 23 March 1741 John Dempster to Richard Ticke of Chestertown in the Province of Maryland, Ship Carpenter - consideration 500 pounds of tobacco - Lott Number Twenty-two in Kingstown. Acknowledged before James Brown and John Earle. Alienation fine, one pence sterling.

401. 1 March 1741 - 23 March 1741 John Dempster to Roger Elston of Kingstown, Planter - consideration 600 pounds of tobacco - Lott Number Six in Kingstown. Wits: James Brown, John Earle. Alienation fine, one pence sterling.

401. 1 March 1741 - 23 March 1741 John Dempster to Henry Cully of Kings Town, Gentleman - consideration &11 current money - Lotts Number Twelve and Thirteen in Kingstown. Alienation fine, two pence.

402. 26 February 1741 - 26 March 1742 Henry Downes, Planter, and Frances his wife, to Richard Costin, Planter - consideration &6.7.0 current money - 22 acres, part of "Carter's Forrest," adjoining "Wilson's Addition," now in the possession of Richard Bennett, and a part of the same tract belonging to John Emerson. Henry and Frances (she being first privately examined) acknowledged before Thomas Wilkinson and Robert Lloyd. Alienation fine, eleven pence sterling.

404. 25 March 1742 - 26 March 1742 Henry Jacobs, Planter, and Anne his wife, to Thomas McClannahan, Planter - consideration 10,000 pounds of tobacco - 100 acres, part of "Fox Harbour," in a fork of Hambleton's Branch next above where Richard Clouds did dwell. Also, part of "Collins Lott," 50 acres on Hambleton's Branch - also 42½ acres, part of "Brotherhood" - on Hambleton's Branch, adjoining "Collins Lott;" "Barton;" "Notlar's Desire" and "Fox Harbour;" devised by William Edwards, deceased, to his daughter Anne, now wife of Henry Jacobs. Henry and Anne (she being first privately examined) acknowledged before Charles Downes and Thomas Wilkinson. Alienation fine, seven shillings, ten pence, half penny sterling. Sig: Ann Jacobs.

406. 27 February 1741 - 1 April 1742 Lavinia Hollingsworth, Widow, who renounced the executorship of the will of Thomas Hollingsworth, Planter, deceased, to Elizabeth Hawkins, Widow and executor of Ernault Hawkins, deceased - in consideration of a balance due to Ernault Hawkins from the estate of Thomas Hollingsworth of &26.12.0 current silver or gold and acquitted by Elizabeth Hawkins, who discharges the said Lavinia from payment - Lavinia, in consideration of the premises and further that Elizabeth Hawkins shall build a

406. 25 foot dwelling house, 15 feet wide where she, Lavinia, shall order, on her father's land; and two cows and calves; and also build
her a cornhouse on the same place next Fall; doth remise, relinq-
uish and quitclaim all her claim to the lands lately sold by Thomas
Hollingsworth to Ernault Hawkins and now in the possession of Elizabeth - particularly, her right of dower. Elizabeth covenants to
have the dwelling built this Spring; deliver the cows and calves by
the last of April next. Wits: Ralph Robotham, Tobias Grisom.
Acknowledged 12 March 1741 before Thomas Hynson Wright and Thomas
Wilkinson.

406. 30 March 1742 - 9 April 1742 Thomas Wilkinson, Gentleman, to Thomas Hynson Wright - consideration ₤40 sterling money of England - a
mulatto woman slave named "Nanny;" a negro boy slave named "Vin"
and a mulatto girl slave called "Rachel." Acknowledged before Robert Norrest Wright and Charles Downes.

407. 31 October 1741 - 8 April 1742 William Wrench, Sr., of St. Paul's
Parish, Planter, to Margaret, wife of James Chaires, daughter of
William Wrench - a gift of love - 200 acres, a moiety of "Wrench's
Farm," separated from the rest by Rowbotham's Branch and now in the
occupation of James Chaires. Wits: Thomas Wilkinson, Charles Neale.
Alienation fine, eight shillings sterling.

408. Recorded 16 April 1742. City and County of Bristol, 9 March 1740.
At a court of Quarter Sessions held in the Guildhall before Henry
Combe, Esquire, Mayor; John Rich, Esquire; and John Blackwell, Aldermen and Justices of the Peace, Thomas Trapp was convicted of a
felony, sentenced to be transported to the colonies for seven years
and to be delivered to Etheldred Davy, Merchant - he giving security for the transportation of the felon.

408. At the Sessions of Goal Delivery held 11 July last, at New Garminn
before Justices Thomas Abney and Thomas Barnett, Richard Pearse and
Earle Burthall were convicted and sentenced to seven years; John
Amor, sentenced to fourteen years. At Warminster, County of Wirts,
16 July last before Richard Willoughby, Edward Ashe, Thomas Bennett
and others, John Spicer, Samuel Bowden, Richard Gay, Jane Haines
and Grace wife of ____ Chappel, were convicted and sentenced to
seven years. James Harris, Edward Hearst, John Eyler, Thomas Cooper, Thomas Bennett of Norton, Thomas Long, Thomas Beath and Matthew
Pitts, Justices of the Peace, nominated Harris, Pitts and Hearst or
any two of them to contract for the transportation of the felons.
Etheldred Davy, Merchant, of the City of Exeter, agreed to transport within three months, 9 September 1741. Edward Holdaway and
Leo. Fletcher, witnessed the contract.

409. 18 July 1741 At a court held for the City and County of Bristol,
before Henry Combe, Mayor; Joseph Jefferis and Arthur Taylor, Aldermen and Justices of the Peace, Margaret Jefferis, Hector Jefferis
and Mary Laure, convicted and sentenced to be transported for seven
years, were assigned to Etheldred Davy.

410. At Brereton, August 1741. Howell John otherwise Blue, of Lanvair - ybrin(?) in the county of Lamarthen, Laborer, was tried and convict- ed on 11 April 1740, of stealing a sorrel mare, the property of Reese Powell and received a sentence of death; William Taylor of Wrexham, County of Denbigh, Yoeman, was tried and convicted of bur- glary and stealing goods out of the house of Samuel Thomas, and was also sentenced to death; Job Pritchard, Yoeman, tried and convicted of stealing a cream coloured mare, property of Elizabeth Cadle, also received a death sentence. Mercy was granted on condition that they be transported for fourteen years to the colonies in America. Moses Jones, late of Cirkhowel, County of Breton, Labourer, convicted of stealing goods of Joel Edmonds, sentenced to be transported for sev- en years. 3 April 1741 Maud Lewis of the Town of Breton, single, convicted of stealing two white linnen aprons, the property of Mary Palfrey, Spinster, also sentenced for seven years. John Hughes, Walter Jeffreys, Howel Gwyn and Richard Williams, Clerk, or any two of them to give the orders for transportation; Hughes, Jeffreys and Williams appointed John Rosser to contract for the transportation and that he take proper security therein, 1 September 1741.

410. Monmouthshire, 16 July 1741 John Rosser, Edward Spencer and William Jenkins, convicted and ordered to be transported to the colonies for seven years. Chapell Hanbury, Charles Vann, Edmund Bradbury, Thomas Evans and Andrew Cuthbert, Justices of the Peace, or any two of them appointed to contract for the transportation, empower William Blow- er, present Goaler of this county to make the contract, 24 August 1741; William Blower assigned to Peter Simons to serve him in Meri- land or some other of His Majesty's colonies, 28 August 1741. Wit: John Legg.

411. Hereford, 13 January 1740. Before Richard Hopton, William Brydges, James Walwyn, Herbert Ambrey, Jr., Thomas Gwyllin, Francis Woodhouse and Roger Hereford, Keepers of the Peace - Thomas Parsons was tried and convicted of felony, and sentenced to the colonies for seven years; the Justices ordered to make contract for this purpose.

411. At the General Quarter Sessions held at the Castle of Exon, County of Devon, 15 July last, Thomas Blackmore, Henry Grater, William Brown and Daniel Jugg, convicted of several felonies, were sentenced to be transported to the colonies for seven years. Sir Henry North- cott, Walter Radcliffe, William Oxenham, Jr. and William Clifford Martyn, ordered to make a contract, assigned the same to Etheldred Davy who obliges to take the convicts to Virginia or some other place within three months of date, 30 September 1741. Thomas Ley, Jr., John Whitehouse, Abigail Taylor and Thomas Ley witnessed for William Clifford Martyn.

412. City and County of Bristol, 7 September 1741, before Henry Combe, Mayor, Joseph Jefferis and Nathaniel Day, Aldermen and Justices of the Peace, Sarah Crow, Sarah Howel, Mary Lovell and Velvidora Davis were convicted of felony and sentenced to be transported for seven years - to be delivered to Etheldred Davy, Merchant.

412. City and County of Bristol, 21 September 1741, before Henry Combe,
      Mayor, Arthur Taylor and Jacob Elton, Aldermen and Justices of the
      Peace, William Morris was convicted of felony and sentenced to be
      transported for seven years to the colonies; delivered to Etheldred
      Davy.

413. City and County of Bristol, 25 August 1741, before Henry Combe,
      Michael Forster and James Denning, Aldermen and Justices of the
      Peace, John Clark and Jonas Wheeler, convicted of felony and senten-
      ced to seven years in the colonies, delivered to Etheldred Davy.

413. Glamorgan, 28 March 1741. At a court held at Cardiff - John Lewis,
      convicted of stealing one linnen shift gown, the goods of Dorothy
      Lewis, sentenced to be transported for seven years; Michael Rich-
      ards, Roger Powell, Roger Powell, the younger, and William Morgan
      or any two of them, shall take out security for his sure and safe
      transportation.

413. Glamorgan, 28 March 1741. Henry Terry, convicted of stealing a
      brass pan, the goods of Elizabeth Davies, Widow - sentenced to be
      transported for seven years - his security assumed by the above.

414. City and County of Exon, 21 September 1741, before Nicholas Lee,
      Mayor, John Belfield, Nathaniel Dowdney, Thomas Copplestone, An-
      thony Tripe, Emanuel Hole, William Habbard, John Newcombe, Matthew
      Spry and Thomas Heath, Aldermen and Justices of the Peace - Eliza-
      beth Crocker, single, was convicted of taking away a silk night gown
      and other goods to the value of ten pence, belonging to Jane Battis-
      hill and also stealing four spring knives, three pair of buckles
      belonging to William Luke, for which she was liable for the punish-
      ment of whipping but was adjudged instead to be transported to the
      colonies for seven years. Etheldred Davy to transport within three
      months and give bond for her security. Wits: Henry Floud, Edmund
      Carwithen.

414. At the Quarter Sessions held at Godwithiel(?) in the County of Corn-
      wall 14 July last, Francis Harris, John Perkin and Anne his wife,
      were convicted of felony and sentenced to be transported for seven
      years. At a Session of Goal Delivery held at Bodwyn, 28 July last,
      John Bennett, Samuel Grey, Anne Raskrogue, convicted of felony, were
      sentenced to be transported for seven years; likewise Elizabeth Long
      for fourteen years. The Court appointed Hugh Piper and Edward Ben-
      nett, Justices of the Peace, to contract for their transportation,
      which agreement was made with Etheldred Davy of the City of Exon -
      to be done within three months, 17 August 1741. John Killiam and
      Francis Kambly witnessed for Hugh Piper; Charles Long and Matthew
      Hawkins for Edward Bennett; John Stoneman and James Rowe, Jr. for
      Etheldred Davy.

415. Hertfordshire, 18 July 1741. At a Court held before Sir William
      Chappell, James Reynolds and Thomas Mulse, Justices of the Peace -
      Richard Morgan, Ann Pritchard, Anthony Howell, Ezekial Pritchard and

415. Mary Williams were tried and convicted; Richard Morgan for robbery
on the highway; Ann Pritchard and Anthony Howell for burglary; Ezekial Pritchard for horse-stealing and Mary Williams for murder - all
sentenced to be transported to the Maryland colony for fourteen
years. Thomas Davis, convicted of grand larceny and liable for punishment of burning in the hand, was ordered to be transported for
seven years. Richard Dausey, Robert Nuett, Roger Hereford, John
Capell, Gridmore(?) Letchmer, Richard Hopton, James Walwyn and Herbert Ambrey the younger, Justices of the Peace, or any two of them,
to make a contract and cause to be delivered to the same.

416. Herefordshire. At the General Delivery of the Goal holden at Hereford, 14 March ____, before William Fortescue, Esquire, Justice of
the court of Common Pleas, Martin Wright, Thomas Mulse and other fellow Justices assigned to deliver the goal of the prisoners therein -
Charles Stokes, Joseph Stocket, Edward Tippens, Thomas Aspy, Thomas
Eliman, Francis Cooper, John Jamison, Thomas Pritchard and William
Gant, convicted of larceny for which they were liable to the punishment of burning in the hand but were orderd to be transported to
the colonies in America for a term of seven years. Richard Dausey,
Robert Nuett, Roger Hereford, John Capell, Richard Hopton, James
Walwyn and Herbert Ambrey the younger, Justices of the Peace, or any
two of them, were appointed to contract for the performance of the
transportation and to order security to be taken.

417. City and County of Bristol, 19 August 1741. At a court held in the
Guildhall before Henry Combe, Mayor, Arthur Taylor and Jacob Elton,
Aldermen and Justices, Mary Thomas, convicted of felony, was sentenced to be transported to the colonies for seven years and to be
delivered to Etheldred Davy, Merchant; he giving security.

417. Robert Hogg the younger, at a Session of Goal Delivery for the County of Devon, held 6 August 1740, was convicted of felony and sentenced to be transported for fourteen years. On 20 July last, Richard
French, Stephen Morey, James Williams, Margaret Warren, Joseph Welsh,
William Beavis, George Poe and William Hogg, convicted of felony,
were sentenced to be transported to the colonies. On 26 March last
the court appointed Robert Stuckey, William Clifford Martyn, William
Hull, Caleb Juglett, George Southcott, William Tucker and Thomas
Balle, Justices of the Peace, or any two of them, to contract for
the performance of transportation amongst others, of the said Robert
Hogg the younger. On 20 July last, the court nominated Sir Henry
Northcote, Robert Stuckey, William Clifford Martin, William Hull,
Caleb Juglett, George Southcott, William Tucker and Thomas Balle,
Justices, to contract for the transportation of Richard French,
Stephen Morey, James Williams, Margaret Warren, Joseph Welsh, Wil-
liam Beavis, George Poe and William Hogg and to order and take care
that such contractors give sufficient security. Thomas Balle and
William Clifford Martyn contracted with Etheldred Davy of the City
of Exon, Merchant, for the transportation of Robert Hogg to Virgin-
ia or some other colony and likewise for the abovenamed other felons.
Davy agreed to transport the prisoners within three months, 2 Octo-

417. ber 1741. John Hampson and Thomas Lley witnessed for Thomas Balle;
Abigail Taylor and Thomas Lley witnessed for William Clifford Martin and Etheldred Davy.

All of the foregoing certificates of Goal Delivery and Transportation were recorded in Queen Ann's County, 16 April 1742.

418. 24 February 1741 - 17 April 1742 Thomas Hynson Wright, Gentleman,
to James Reed, Yoeman - consideration 3,500 pounds of tobacco - 50
acres, part of "Providence," lying near the main road leading from
Collins' Mill to Kings Town. Wits: James Tilghman, Lambert Wickes.
Acknowledged before Robert Norrest Wright and Robert Lloyd. Alienation fine, see f. 428.

420. 7 April 1742 - 28 April 1742 John Punny, Planter, to Robert Norrest
Wright - consideration ₤20 current money and 9,000 pounds of tobacco-
part of three tracts called "Claxon Hills," "Jones'es Parke" and
"Norrest's Addition," lying at the head of a branch formerly called
Matthais' Branch and containing 125 acres. Acknowledged before
Robert Lloyd and John Earle. See f. 428 for receipt of alienation.

421. 8 May 1742 John Dempster, Gentleman, to Richard Tilghman - consideration ₤230 current - 498 acres of land on Fishing Creek, part of
"Poplar Hill" (except that part laid out for Kings Town). Acknowledged before Thomas Hynson Wright and Charles Downes.

423. 10 May 1742 - 15 May 1742 An indenture tripartite between Esther
Devonish of Kent County, Province of Maryland, single, a daughter
and co-heir of Robert Devonish, late of the same county, deceased,
of the first part; Martha Devonish, single, another daughter of same
Robert Devonish of the second part and Robert Devonish of Kent County, Planter, of the third part - in consideration of twenty shillings paid to each, Esther and Martha release an undivided two-
fourths part and shares of the land called "Lambeth." Reference to
a grant made 7 March 1688 to Robert Devonish the grandfather of Esther and Martha, of "Lambeth," 250 acres in a small fork of Unicorn
Branch, which Robert in a will written 9 April 1699 devised for life
to his then daughter Elizabeth after whose death the same tract descended to the aforesaid Robert the father as heir at law to the
same Robert, the grantee which said Robert, father of Esther and
Martha, dyed intestate leaving female issue only, i.e. Esther, Martha, Hannah and Sarah to whom the land descended in copartnership
and still remains undivided. Wits: Eliza Miller, S. Knight. Acknowledged before S. Knight, Justice of the Provincial Court.

424. 11 May 1742 - 20 May 1742 Richard Bennett, Esquire, to Edward Tilghman, Gentleman - in consideration of ₤9.4.1½ current silver and
2,361 pounds of tobacco - part of "Coursey Upon Wye," mortgaged by
William Turbutt, 6 March 1721 in consideration of ₤232.16.0 and
24,030 pounds of tobacco; and by the will of Coll. William Coursey
given to his wife, Elizabeth; which is all that part lying on the
east side of Carroll's Cove, Wye River, containing 600 acres; the

424. part conveyed lies within the lines of part of the mortgaged land
given by William Turbutt to Edward Tilghman by a deed of gift - the
whole forfeited to Richard Bennett. This deed of release acknowledged before Robert Norrest Wright and Robert Lloyd.

426. 27 April 1742 - 20 May 1742 Solomon Wyatt, Planter, and Margarett
his wife, to John Nevill, Planter - consideration 3,000 pounds of
tobacco - 200 acres, part of "Tilghman's Discovery," lying on the
east side of Double Creek - the dower of Mary Andrews, Solomon's
mother, only excepted during her natural life. Solomon and Margarett (she being first privately examined) acknowledged before James
Brown and Dowdall Thompson.

428. 17 April 1742 Richard Tilghman to James Reed - receipt for two
shillings sterling, alienation fine.

428. 28 April 1742 Richard Tilghman to Robert Norrest Wright - receipt
for two shillings sterling, alienation fine.

428. 1 March 1741 - 27 May 1742 Charles Hynson of Chester Towne, Merchant, to Richard Bennett - reference to a deed made 18 October
1737 between Richard Howell of the City of Philadelphia, Merchant,
and Letitiah his wife, to Charles Hynson, for 500 acres of land
laid out for Cornelius Comegys at the head of Chester River and
called "Poplar Plaines." To be held by Hynson in trust to sell, de-
mise or mortgage as he thinks fit; he to raise ₤24.2.0 current
money and ₤8.8.6 sterling money of Great Britain and 18,362 pounds
of tobacco with interest, to pay a debt due Bennett from Richard
Howell and a certain William Chanceller - the surplus to be paid to
Howell. Richard Howell has agreed since with Richard Bennett for
the land in discharge for part of the money and tobacco to the value of ₤30 sterling and ordered Hynson to make over the land. Acknowledged before James Brown and John Earle. Alienation fine, twenty shillings sterling, paid to Richard Tilghman.

430. 11 May 1742 - 3 June 1742 Richard Bennett to Nathan Wright and
Mary his wife, one of the daughters of Major William Turbutt, deceased - part of "Coursey Upon Wye," mortgaged by William Turbutt
to Bennett, 6 March 1721, and devised to Mary by his last will and
testament. Acknowledged before Robert Norrest Wright and Robert
Lloyd.

431. 10 June 1742 Thomas Davis, Planter, to Richard Tilghman - mortgage of ₤120 current money, due by 10 June 1745, on part of land
called "Content" and a negro lad named "Teago." Acknowledged before Thomas Hynson Wright and Robert Norrest Wright.

433. 14 June 1742 William Anderson, Commander of the ship "Crighton,"
anchored in Chester River and bound to London, will take tobacco on
board at the rate of ₤9 sterling per tonn, consigned to James Buchanan, Merchant in London.

433. 16 June 1742 Richard Tilghman to William Wilkinson - receipt for two shillings sterling, alienation fine on deed RT A f.309.

434. 1 June 1742 - 21 June 1742 Robert Wharton als Warton, Planter, of the first part; Thomas Honey of the second part and William Robinson, Planter, of the third - indenture tripartite. Reference here to the patent on "Highgate Lane," granted 8 May 1683 to Michael Hackett - on the south side of the Southeast Branch, adjoining land laid out for Henry Parker called "Parker's Lott," 100 acres. On 15 November Michael Hackett sold to Daniel Dempsey under whom William Robinson claims a title therein as the son and heir at law of Margarett Dempsey who was the only child and heir of the said Daniel. Robert Wharton has part by a deed from William Bolton who claimed under William Hollingsworth, he claiming the right by virtue ot a sale to him from Thomas Honey which he pretended to have title to by virtue of a purchase from Michael Hackett. To settle "Highgate Lane" and recover one other parcel of land called "Wharton's Marsh," contiguous to the first tract, granted 6 November 1725 to Robert Wharton - supposedly a part of "Highgate Lane," in consideration of 11,000 pounds of tobacco paid to Robert Wharton, 3,000 pounds paid to William Robinson and five shillings to Thomas Honey, the three above convey to the Reverend Arthur Holt, Rector of St. Luke's Parish. John Prior and George Barkhurst witnessed Thomas Honey's receipt to Holt for five shillings. Acknowledged before Robert Norrest Wright and John Earle by all three grantors and at the same time also appeared Anne, wife of William Robinson and Sarah, wife of Thomas Honey, who were examined privately. Alienation fine, five shillings sterling and one pence, paid to Richard Tilghman.

437. 24 May 1742 - 21 June 1742 James Hollyday, Gentleman, to John Hawkins, Jr. and Sarah his wife - consideration £166 current money - part of "Macklinborough," now in the possession of Edward Brown and Mary his wife, mother of the said Sarah and whereon Edward and Mary Brown do dwell - bound by part of the land belonging to James Hollyday and on the northeast by a parcel now in the possession of John Hawkins, father of John, being part of his dwelling plantation; and on the northwest by the river - containing 90 acres, mortgaged to Hollyday by Hawkins, 3 April 1739. Acknowledged before James Brown and John Earle. Alienation fine, one shilling, nine pence, one-half penny sterling.

438. 19 April 1742 - 21 June 1742 Richard Hynson to Lawrence Copland - a lease for part of "Ann's Portion," lying eastward of the dwelling plantation of Richard Hynson and near the head of Willson's Branch - for a term of seven years from 1 January last paying one ear of Indian Corn the first two years and every year after, 600 pounds of tobacco. Hynson to build one 30-foot tobacco house this ensuing summer; Lawrence to plant 100 apple trees and keep fenced from cattle or other creatures. Acknowledged before John Earle and D. Thompson.

439. 16 June 1742 - 21 June 1724 Josiah Coleman and Rachel his wife, of Kings Town, Innholder, to Henry Cully, Merchant of Kings Town and

439. John Collins - consideration ₺53 current - Lott Number Eleven in Kings Town. Acknowledged before James Brown and D. Thompson. Alienation fine three farthings paid to Richard Tilghman.

440. 1 February 1741 - 22 June 1742 Nathaniel Scott, Planter, to John Nabb, Planter - consideration 2,000 pounds of tobacco - 40 acres, part of "Marshy Creek," lying on the east side of Tuckahoe Creek, originally 100 acres granted to Scott by patent dated 28 May 1723 - near Lowe's Marsh and adjoining Falkner's part. Acknowledged before William Jumpe and Thomas Wilkinson.

441. 13 February 1741 - 22 June 1742 Benjamin Falconer, Jacob Falconer and Isaac Falconer, of Dorchester County, Planters, to John Nabb, Planter - consideration ₺30 Maryland currency - 60 acres, part of "Marshy Creek als Crook," originally 100 acres granted to Nathaniel Scott, 28 May 1723. The part conveyed was sold to Benjamin Falconer, Sr. and by his last will and testament left to his sons Benjamin, Jacob and Isaac. Acknowledged before Thomas Hynson WRight and Charles Downes.

443. 11 May 1742 - 22 June 1742 Richard Bennett to Thomas Harris - release of Elizabeth Harris's part of "Coursey Upon Wye" - mortgaged to Bennett, 16 March 1721 by William Turbutt, father of Elizabeth Harris, and devised to his wife Elizabeth Coursey for 600 acres - all on the east side of Carroll's Cove, Wye River.'
11 May 1742 Richard Bennett to Thomas Harris - receipt for ₺399.16. current money in consideration of the above land. Acknowledged before Robert Norrest Wright and Robert Lloyd.

444. 20 April 1742 - 22 June 1742 Thomas Shoebruks, Planter, and Margret his wife, to Archibald Greenfield, Mariner - consideration ₺32 current - three lotts with the houses thereon in Ogletown - Numbers Thirty-eight; Thirty-nine and Fifty-nine. Wits: Ernault Hawkins, William Bishop. Thomas and Margret his wife (she being first privately examined) acknowledged before James Browne and John Earle. Alienation fine, two pence farthings sterling.

445. 15 March 1741 - 22 June 1742 Richard Turbutt, son of Samuel, Gentleman, to John Baggs - releases 22 acres of land near the head of Choptank River behind Oldtown, called "Controversy" - devised by Samuel Turbutt to be made over to Baggs in exchange for two parcels of land called "Blissland" and "Baggs' Marsh." Wits: Thomas Bullen, Rachel Bullen. Acknowledged before Risdon Bozman and Thomas Bullen - certified as Justices of the Peace by John Leeds, Clerk of Talbot County. Alienation fine, eleven pence sterling.

447. 28 June 1742 Christopher Wilkinson to Richard Tilghman - consideration ₺153.1.0 current - mortgages eight slaves, "Cesar," "Ben," "Sam," "Hagar," "Mareah," "Nan," "Jack" and "Will," with all of their increase; also a plow horse called "Dover" and a ball horse that was formerly John Nabb's; two 5-year old steers, four heiffers, 3 years old; three sows and yearlings; one cow and calf; twelve head of sheep.

447. (Marks given). The mortgage due on or before 1 October 1743. Acknowledged before John Earle.

448. 8 July 1742 Richard Tilghman to John Nevill - receipt for four shillings sterling, alienation fine for deed on folio 426 and 427.

448. 1 February 1741 - 7 July 1742 Thomas Hynson Wright to his daughter, Mary Ann, wife of William Hopper - a gift of love - 200 acres, part of "Guilford," bought of Susanna Gillaspie; also "Dantin," 210 acres according to patent and part of "Coursey's Point" otherwise "Smith's Mistake" in Spaniard's Neck; lately bought of William Bishop for 200 acres, where William Saunders now dwells. Acknowledged before James Brown and Humphery Wells, Jr.

448. 30 March 1742 - 17 July 1742 Thomas Wilkinson, Gentleman, to Thomas Hynson Wright, Gentleman - consideration ₤20 sterling - 100 acres, part of "Providence," on the north side of Corsica Creek being the plantation whereon William Smith now dwells. Acknowledged before Robert N. Wright and Charles Downes. Alienation fine two shillings sterling, paid to Richard Tilghman.

450. 28 January 1741 - 17 July 1742 Thomas Bartlet the younger, of Talbot County, Planter, and Mary his wife, to Samuel Bartlet of Queen Ann's County, Blacksmith, and Rachel his wife - 100 acres, part of "Ratcliffe Mannour" in St. Michaels Parish of Talbot County; now in the possession of Thomas Bartlet the elder and whereon he now dwells, (which same parcel Thomas the elder and Margaret his wife deeded to Thomas the younger this date) - in exchange for part of a tract to be given by Samuel and Rachel his wife to Thomas, the younger; 120 acres, part of "Turner's Plains Addition," in Tuckahoe Neck and now in Samuel's possession and whereon he now dwells, given by Edward Turner, deceased, to Rachel Bartlet. Wits: W. Thomas, Robert Goldsborough, Jr. On 26 January 1741 Thomas, Mary, Samuel and Rachel (Mary and Rachel being first privately examined) acknowledged before Perry Benson and W. Thomas. Certified by John Leeds, Clerk, as Justices of Talbot County. 10 July 1742 Richard Tilghman to Thomas Bartlet, Jr. - receipt for four shillings, ten pence sterling, alienation fine for "Turner's Plains Addition."

452. 15 July 1742 Thomas Harris brought an account of William Turbutt's mortgage payments to be recorded. (Detailed and itemized).

453. 15 July 1742 - 12 August 1742 William Finney of Talbot County, Planter, to John Hall, Planter - consideration 11,250 pounds of tobacco - 300 acres, part of "Dance" at the head of Frenchwoman's Branch of Tuckahoe Creek. Acknowledged before Thomas Hynson Wright and Charles Downes. Alienation fine, twelve shillings sterling.

456. 2 July 1742 - 24 August 1742 Richard Bennett, Merchant, to William Newnam, Planter - consideration 10,000 pounds of tobacco to be paid in three years - "Shaver," on Unicorne Branch, originally surveyed for Francis Sheppard for 200 acres. Sheppard conveyed to Frances

37.

456.   Mitchell, 21 June 1687, the deed recorded in Talbot County; and by
        Robert Taylor and Frances aforesaid, his then wife, conveyed to Rich-
        ard Bennett. Wits: Robert Gordon, William Carmichall. Acknowledged
        before Robert Gordon, Justice of the Provincial Court. Alienation
        fine, eight shillings sterling, paid to Richard Tilghman.

457.   14 July 1742 - 25 August 1742 John Hawkins, Jr. and Sarah his wife,
        to Edward Brown - consideration ₤106 current money and 5,000 pounds
        of tobacco - 100 acres, part of "Macklinborough," adjoining the part
        sold to James Hollyday in 1724 - on the main road that leads from
        Ogletown down the county - on Dividing Creek. John and Sarah (she
        being first privately examined) acknowledged before Thomas Wilkinson
        and John Earle. Alienation fine, three shillings sterling.

459.   25 August 1742 John Errickson, son of Charles Errickson of Kent Is-
        land, Planter, to Thomas Marsh, Gentleman - consideration 2,500
        pounds of tobacco - 150 acres called "Mary's Portion," lately lying
        in Kent County but according to the late division now in Queen Ann's
        near the middle of Kent Island - adjoining the land of Richard Blunt
        and Phillip Connyer. Beginning at the head of Tarrkill Creek - runs
        to the head of Martin's Creek - adjoining Phillip Conyer's land
        known by the name of Broad Creek land. From Tarrkill Field runs
        straight to the first tree. Acknowledged before Robert Norrest
        Wright and John Earle. Alienation fine, six shillings sterling.

460.   14 September 1742 - 16 September 1742 Henry Cully and John Collins
        to John Hart, Innholder - consideration ₤53 current money - Lott Num-
        ber Eleven in Kings Town. Henry Cully and his wife Christian,(she
        being first privately examined) acknowledged before Thomas Wilkinson
        and James Brown.

461.   1 June 1742 - 22 October 1742 Burgess Watson, heir at law to Francis
        Watson, to Morgan Ponder - consideration 2,000 pounds of tobacco -
        50 acres called "Watson's Desire," in the Long Neck near the Long
        Marsh. Acknowledged before James Brown and John Earle. Alienation
        fine, two shillings sterling.

463.   19 October 1742 Thomas Reed, Master of the ship "Mary," lying at
        anchor in Wye River, bound from thence to London, will take tobacco
        on board on freight at ₤9 sterling, consigned to James Buchanan of
        London, Merchant.

463.   10 October 1742 - 28 October 1742 Charles Lowder, Planter, to Fran-
        cis Rochester - consideration ₤4.2.0 current money - one iron pott;
        one pail and piggon; four hoes; two iron wedges; (one plowshare, two
        colters and all tackling); one pewter dish; one stock lock; one coop-
        er's 'adds'; one joynter stock and two irons; one joyner's hatchet;
        one iron compass; one broad ax and all tobacco now on the plantation
        on ye tract called "Lowder's Hazard." Wits: Humphery Wells, Jr.,
        Charles Lizenbe.

463.   20 September 1742 - 28 October 1742 Charles Lowder and Ann his wife,

463. to Francis Rochester - consideration 13,000 pounds of tobacco - 77
acres, "Lowder's Hazard," lying on the north side of Chapple Road,
north side Red Lyon Branch. Wits: Richard Wells, Jr., James Maud.
Charles and Ann (she being first privately examined) acknowledged
before James Brown and Humphery Wells, Jr. Alienation fine, three
shillings, one pence sterling paid to Richard Tilghman.

465. 9 November 1742 Christopher Wilkinson, Gentleman, to Richard Tilghman - consideration £166.1.0 current money and £40.19.11 sterling
money of Great Britain - mortgages eight negroes, i.e. "Cesar als
Tom;" "Ben;" "Sam;" "Hagar;" "Mareah;" "Nan;" "Jack" and "Will;" a
plow horse called "Dover;" a ball horse formerly John Nabb's; a
horse called "Dragon;" three mares; one 4-year old horse and four
2-year old colts; twelve head of sheep; two 5-year old steers; six
cows; four heiffers, 4 years old; three heiffers, 3 years old; two
heiffers, 2 years old; one calf; forty head of hoggs; also three
featherbeds and furniture; six _____ ; one chest of drawers; one
smaller ditto; one dozen chairs and all of my pewter - payment due
on or before 1 October 1743. Wits: Thomas Wilkinson, John Tilden,
Jr.

466. 9 November 1742 Richard Tilghman's receipts for alienation fines:
to John Nabb for two shillings, five pence sterling,
to John Nabb for one shilling, seven pence sterling,
to Richard Harrington for two shillings sterling, folio 386.

466. 26 August 1742 - 22 November 1742 Richard Wells, Jr. and Mary his
wife, to John MacConnikind of Kent County on Delaware, Province of
Pensilvania, Planter - consideration £310 current - 200 acres,
"Wood Ridge" - on Wallis's Branch and Wallis's Marsh, 100 perches
east of a small path leading from Francis Spry's to John Hamer's;
also 100 acres adjoining, called "Wood Ridg Addition." Richard and
Mary (she being first privately examined) acknowledged before Robert Lloyd and Humphery Wells, Jr. Alienation fine, twelve shillings sterling paid to Richard Tilghman.

468. 7 August 1742 - 23 November 1742 Edward Cox of Baltimore County,
Planter, to John Halloway of Baltimore County, Planter - consideration 1,500 pounds of tobacco - 400 acres on Kent Island called
"Little Ease." Wits: T. Sheredine, Geer Buchanan. Edward Cox and
Nissey his wife(she being first privately examined) acknowledged the
deed before Sheredine and Buchanan, Justices of the Peace for Baltimore County and at the same time Nissey Cox relinquished her right
of dower. Certified by T. Brerewood, Clerk of BAltimore County.
Alienation fine, eight shillings sterling, paid to R. Tilghman.

469. 29 October 1742 - 24 November 1742 Charles Lizenby, Planter, to
James Scotten - consideration 1,600 pounds of tobacco - 50 acres,
part of "Tom's Fancy Enlarged," lying in Tully's Neck adjoining a
part sold to John Lloyd and a part sold to Nathaniel Read. Wits:
James Mackey, Thomas Walker, A. Barry. C. Lizenby to Francis Rochester - Power of Attorney to acknowledge the deed - before Robert

469. Norrest Wright and Associate Justices. Alienation fine two shill-
      ings sterling paid to Richard Tilghman.

471. 13 December 1742 - 13 January 1742 Anthony Roe and Jane his wife,
      to Henry Casson - consideration 6,500 pounds of tobacco - 100 acres
      called "Dudley's Desire," on the east side of Tuckahoe Creek - ad-
      joining "Jump's Lane," formerly laid out for William Jumpe. Anthony
      and Jane (she being first privately examined) acknowledged before
      William Jumpe and Thomas Wilkinson. Alienation fine, four shillings
      sterling.

472. 7 January 1742 - 20 January 1742 Patrick Boon and Mary his wife, to
      Giles Hicks - consideration 4,600 pounds of tobacco - 100 acres,
      part of "Killcray" in Tuckahoe Neck - adjoining Thomas Meeds.
      Patrick and Mary (she being first privately examined) acknowledged
      before William Jumpe and Henry Casson. Alienation fine, four shill-
      ings sterling.

473. 22 December 1742 - 20 January 1742 William Scott and Jane his wife,
      to Anthony Roe - consideration 6,000 pounds of tobacco - 100 acres,
      part of "Sawyer's Range" - on the south side of Red Lyon Branch.
      William and Jane (she being first privately examined) acknowledged
      before James Brown and Dowdall Thompson.

474. 16 December 1742 - 27 January 1742 Thomas Roe, Planter, to Henry
      Feddeman, Gentleman - consideration 13,000 pounds of tobacco - 100
      acres, part of "Hackett's Garden," on the east side of Tuckahoe
      Creek - now in the possession of Henry Feddeman. Wits: William
      Jumpe and Henry Casson. Alienation fine, four shillings sterling.

476. 18 August 1742 - 3 February 1742 Robert Devonish, Planter, of Kent
      County, Province of Maryland, and Hannah his wife, to James Claypole
      of Chester Town, Kent County, Tanner - in consideration of ₤40 cur-
      rent money and 6,000 pounds of tobacco - three-fourths part of "Lam-
      beth;" two-fourths granted to Robert by Esther and Martha Devonish
      and one-fourth belonging to him and Hannah his wife in her own right
      as a co-heir of Robert Devonish, the father, deceased - the said
      Robert, the father, dying and left Esther, Martha and Hannah and
      Mary, his heirs. Wits: S. Knight, Annis Knight. Robert and Han-
      nah acknowledged their deed before S. Knight, a Justice of the Pro-
      vincial Court (Hannah being first privately examined).

478. 14 January 1742 - 3 February 1742 John Hollingsworth, Planter, to
      Richard Porter, Jr., Chirurgeon - consideration ₤175 current - the
      plantation "whereon I lately dwelt, formerly in Talbot County, now
      Queen Ann's," - lying on the east branch of Chester River; part of
      "Annthrop," originally granted to William Hemsley - all remaining
      after the part sold to William Campbell. A mortgage due within
      three years from this date. John and Elizabeth his wife (she being
      first privately examined) acknowledged before James Brown and Dow-
      dall Thompson.

479. 10 January 1742 - 3 February 1742 Michael Hussey, Planter, and
Margaret his wife, to George Baynard, Planter - consideration 7,000
pounds of tobacco - all the land of Michael Hussey, Sr. devised to
his son John Hussey, late of Queen Ann's County, 18 April 1733;
which descended to Michael Hussey (Jr.) as the heir of his brother.
Michael and Margaret (she being first privately examined) acknowledged before William Jumpe and Henry Casson. Alienation fine,
seven shillings, four pence, half penny sterling paid to Richard
Tilghman.

481. 5 February 1742 - 12 February 1742 Hannah Phillips, Jr. to Edward
Downes - consideration five shillings - one negro girl called
"Judey." Wits: Sarah Brown, Edward Brown.

7 February 1742 Edward Downes to Henry Jacobs - consideration ₤25
paper money and 2,000 pounds of tobacco. Wit: Daniel Griffith.

481. 8 February 1742 Dorcas Holt, Widow, to her daughter-in-law, Rebecca
Holt, Widow, and her grandchildren Arthur and James Hynson Holt,
sons of Rebecca - in consideration of natural love and affection
and payment of 3,000 pounds of tobacco yearly during her life -
conveys negro slaves, George, Sipio, Chloe, and Phillis; and all
her goods, chattels, plate, household stuff, money, debts, dues
and demands; either in her own right or as executor or administra-
tor of her late husband, Joseph Holt, deceased. George and Sipio
to Arthur holt at age twenty-one; Chloe and Phillis to James Hynson
Holt at age twenty-one. Rebecca Holt to have Power of Attorney to
settle all accounts. Acknowledged before James Brown and Dowdall
Thompson.

482. 1 September 1742 - 22 February 1742 Peter Froom, Blacksmith, and
Elizabeth his wife, both of Prince William County, Parish of Truro,
Colony of Virginia, to John Awbrey, Thomas Awbrey, Richard Awbrey,
executors of Francis Awbrey, Gentleman, deceased, of the said county and Parish - in consideration of ₤60 - 179 acres, part of "Prophecy," lying on the west side of the southwest branch of Island Creek
formerly sold by William Marsh and conveyed to James Earle, Sr. by
a deed for 400 acres, dated 26 September 1726 - adjoining "Waterford," laid out for Andrew Skinner and Nathaniel Evitt and now possessed by William Austin; and adjoining "Readbourn," possessed by
James Hollyday and where he now lives. Also 38 acres more, part of
100 acres which James Earle, Sr. bought of Francis Cole and being
part of "Prophecy;" also "Heath's Discovery," 23 acres adjoining
"Larrington," formerly taken up by John Broadribb and adjoining
"Prophecy," formerly taken up by Daniel Jenifer - which 23 acres was
bought of James Paul Heath by James Earle, Sr., 7 February 1733 and
it was patented by James Paul Heath, 1 November 1701. All three
tracts to contain 240 acres of land. Wits: Ninian Beall, Nathan
Peddycoart.

Prince George's County, Maryland. 1 September 1742 Peter and Eliza-

482. beth Froom acknowledged before Nathaniel Wickham, Jr. and James Edmonston, Justices of the Peace (Elizabeth being first privately examined out of hearing of her husband). The Justices certified by Thomas Lee, Clerk. 19 February 1742 Richard Tilghman to Thomas Awbrey - receipt for nine shillings, seven pence, half penny sterling, alienation fine.

485. 9 October 1742 - 5 February 1742 Elizabeth Fiddeman, Widow and Relict of Philemon Fiddeman, Gentleman, to her son Henry Fiddeman - 55 acres called "Large Range" and "Háckett's Garden," her possession for life. Henry hath contracted with John Maine, Merchant, Factor and Attorney for Etheldred Davy of the City and County of Exon, Kingdom of Great Britain, for the sale of the fee simple and his inheritance of the land and her right of dower - she being willing to perfect the contract. Acknowledged before William Jumpe and Henry Casson. Alienation fine, two shillings, two pence, half penny sterling.

486. 26 October 1742 - 5 February 1742 Isaac Payne, Planter, and Sarah his wife, to John Maine, Merchant - consideration 7,000 pounds of tobacco - 150 acres, called "New London," on the east side of Tuckahoe Creek, adjoining the land formerly laid out for James Eustace. On 11 September 1733 James Daulton gave this land to Isaac Payne, his friend. Isaac and Sarah (she being first privately examined) acknowledged before William Jumpe and Henry Casson. Alienation fine, six shillings, sterling paid to Richard Tilghman.

488. 26 October 1742 - 5 February 1742 An indenture tripartite between John Baynard, Gentleman; John Mayne, Merchant, Factor and Attorney for Etheldred Davy, and Etheldred Davy. In consideration of ₤49 and five guineas paid by John Mayne for Etheldred Davy - conveys parts of two tracts of land called "Large Range" and "Baynard's Large Range" - 49 acres adjoining "Hackett's Garden." Acknowledged before William Jumpe and Henry Casson. Alienation fine, one shilling, eleven pence. half penny sterling.

491. 26 October 1742 - 5 February 1742 Henry Feddeman, Planter, to Etheldred Davy, City and County of Exon, Kingdom of Great Britain - in consideration of ₤55 current money - 55 acres, part of "Large Range" and "Hackett's Garden." Warranted against any heirs under Richard Feddeman, deceased, (late grandfather of Henry Feddeman). Henry Feddeman to Etheldred Davy - Receipt of ₤55 by the hand of John Mayne, Factor. Acknowledged before William Jumpe and Henry Casson. Alienation fine, two shillings, two pence, half penny sterling.

493. 10 February 1742 - 17 February 1742 James Williams and Phebe his wife, Robert Smith and Rachel his wife, to William Smith - consideration 6,500 pounds of tobacco - 200 acres called "Salisbury Plains" - adjoining "Walnut Ridge." James and Phebe (she being first privately examined) acknowledged before Robert Norrest Wright and Thomas Wilkinson. Alienation fine, eight shillings sterling.

495. 22 September 1742 - 22 February 1742 Joseph Merchant, Planter, to

495.   James Knotts, Planter - consideration 3,000 pounds of tobacco - 50 acres of land called "Littleworth," lying on the Island Marsh and the Short Marsh issuing out of Tuckahoe Creek. Warranted against the dower of Rebecca, wife of John Lloyd. Acknowledged before William Jumpe and Henry Casson. Alienation fine, two shillings sterling.

497.   20 December 1742 - 23 February 1742 William Bishop, Gentleman, to Thomas Hynson Wright and William Hopper, Gentlemen - in consideration of ₤452 current money - mortgages the remaining part unsold of 520 acres called "Smith's Mistake" on Corsica Creek; also six negroes: "Acqua," "Nan," "Esther," "Sarah," "Beck," and a boy named "Acqua." Wits: Vincent Vanderford, Daniel Griffith. Acknowledged before Charles Downes and Thomas Wilkinson.

498.   15 February 1742 An agreement of division to be made in case Bishop does not redeem the above property - mention of Mary Ann Hopper, wife of William Hopper. Wits: Charles Moor, John Davis, Jr.

498.   3 March 1742 - 4 March 1742 Richard Lee, Planter, to Thomas Price, Planter - consideration 1,804 pounds of tobacco - all of the tobacco in the tobacco house where I now live; one featherbed and furniture; one heiffer, three years old and a red yearling (marks given); two sows; seven piggs; two iron potts and potthooks; two broad hoes; two narrow hoes; one broad ax; one narrow ax. Acknowledged before Thomas Wilkinson and Henry Casson.

499.   23 February 1742 - 16 February 1742 "Then received from Mrs. Frances Elbert, a note of credit to Mr. William Carmichall for the sum of 682 pounds of tobacco, which with 82 pounds of tobacco that I'm indebted to her on account, I doe hereby acknowledge to receive in full satisfaction for my third part or share of the crop of tobacco made on the plantation where I was overseer last year." David Baily. Wit: Jere. Grasingham. Acknowledged 16 February before Robert Lloyd.

499.   3 December 1742 - 24 February 1742 John Swift, Planter, and Anne his wife, to Thomas Sands - consideration 6,000 pounds of tobacco - 70 acres called "Timber Ridge," lying between Red Lyon and Unicorne Branches - adjoining Thomas Bestwick's land - also 23 acres, part of "Swift's Outlett," lying between the two branches, adjoining "Northumberland." John and Anne (she being first privately examined) acknowledged before James Brown and Dowdall Thompson. Alienation fine, three shillings, eight pence, half-penny sterling.

500.   24 February 1742 William Murphy and Eleanor his wife, Planter, to John Legg, Planter - consideration ₤50 paper money and 500 pounds of tobacco and four shillings sterling - a tract of land called "Oldson's Relief," formerly surveyed and granted to John Oldson for 100 acres - on Kent Island, adjoining the "Barren Ridge" and "Limerick," laid out for John Dine; and "Cooper's Quarter." Wits: Joseph Sudler, Charles Browne. William and Eleanor (she being first privately exam-

43.

500. ined) acknowledged before William Jumpe and Joseph Sudler. Alienation fine, four shillings, sterling, paid to Richard Tilghman.

502. 21 September 1742 - 24 February 1742 Nathaniel Read and Sarah his
wife, to Matthew Read - "Whereas Matthew Read, formerly of Talbot
County, deceased, (father of the above Nathaniel and grandfather of
Matthew), devised to his two sons, Matthew and Nathaniel, all of
"Reading" to be divided - and after it was found to include a considerable quantity of navigable water, Nathaniel and Matthew request-
ed a special warrant for a resurvey called "New Reading;" but before
the patent was issued, Matthew died, leaving a son, the above Matt-
hew (a minor), heir at law to his father; the patent was then grant-
ed to Nathaniel, who now agrees to a division in consideration that
Matthew and Henrietta his wife, hath made over the remaining part of
"New Reading" - gives a quitclaim to the part on Read's Creek, now
Wright's Creek, up to the Deep Branch and the exterior of the tract."
Acknowledged before Robert Norrest Wright and Charles Downes.

503. 26 February 1742 Richard Bennett, Gentleman, to Matthew Tilghman of
Talbot County, Gentleman - consideration ₤30 sterling - part of
"Poplar Plains," lying in the woods at the head of the Chester River,
originally surveyed for Cornelius Comegys for 500 acres - sold to
Bennett by Charles Hynson of Kent County to whom it was conveyed by
Richard Howell of Philadelphia and Letitia his wife, one of the
daughters of Coll. Edward Scott of Kent County, in' trust to impower
him to convey the same to some purchaser; this part being 191 acres.
Wits: Thomas Wilkinson, R. Porter. Acknowledged before Thomas Wilkinson and Robert Lloyd. Alienation fine, seven shillings, eight
pence, sterling.

504. 12 January 1742 - 1 May 1742 Ernault Hawkins and Jane his wife, to
Thomas Baily, Jr., son of Jacob Baily - consideration 1,500 pounds
of tobacco - 25 acres, part of "Larinton" - on the southwest branch
of Island Creek. Ernault and Jane acknowledged before Robert Norrest Wright and John Earle (Jane being first privately examined).
Alienation fine, one shilling, sterling.

506. 4 November 1742 - 16 March 1742 Alice Collier, Widow, to her daughter, Margaret Carter - a gift of love - 100 acres, part of "Bishop's
Addition" and "Bishop's Outlett" - on Corsica Creek. Acknowledged
before James Brown and John Earle. Alienation fine, four shillings,
sterling, paid to Richard Tilghman.

506. 26 February 1742 - 28 February 1742 Elizabeth Hawkins, Widow and
Relict of Coll. Ernault Hawkins, to Richard Bennett, Merchant -
consideration ₤100 current - two tracts of land mortgaged by James
Knowles to Ernault Hawkins, vizt: "Ulthorpe," originally granted to
Ralph Page for 100 acres; the other, "Wright's Chance," originally
surveyed for Samuel Wright for 124 acres. Acknowledged before Robert Lloyd and Humphery Wells, Jr.

508. 22 November 1742 - 23 March 1742 Grace Woodward of Talbot County, one of the heiresses of Robert Jones, late of Talbot, Planter, deceased; who made no will but left issue, Grace and Elizabeth, his only children, to Edward Neall of Talbot County, Planter - consideration ₤15 current money - one-half of "Shadwell Addition" formerly conveyed to her father by Thomas Turner and Sarah his wife, late of Talbot - containing 50 acres. Wits: T. Bullen, James Wrightson, Elizabeth Spence. Acknowledged before Thomas Bozman and Thomas Bullen who were certified as Justices of Talbot County by John Leeds, Clerk. Alienation fine, two shillings sterling.

509. 4 March 1742 - 23 March 1742 William Jumpe, Gentleman, and Susanna his wife, to William Barrick of Talbot County, Planter - consideration 4,500 pounds of tobacco - 50 acres called "Jumpe's Choice" - lying in Tuckahoe in Queen Ann's County, patented to his father by Lord Baltimore and lately held by Thomas Jumpe, Jr. under the said William - lying southwest of John Wooters's plantation, being the other 50 acres in the patent. William and Susanna (she being first privately examined) acknowledged before Thomas Wilkinson and Henry Casson. Alienation fine, two shillings sterling, paid to Richard Tilghman.

510. 24 March 1742 William Osburn of Kent Island, Planter, to John Smyth - consideration ₤40 current money - 100 acres on Kent Island called "Timber Neck" - at the head of Pigg Quarter Creek. Acknowledged before Thomas Wilkinson and Joseph Sudler. Alienation fine, two shillings, sterling.

512. 24 March 1742 William Parker, Planter, to Thomas Price - consideration 6,000 pounds of tobacco - 100 acres, part of "Chestnut Meadow." Acknowledged before William Jumpe and James Brown. Alienation fine, four shillings sterling, paid to Richard Tilghman.

513. 16 March 1742 - 24 March 1742 Henry Wilcocks to his son, James Wilcocks - consideration 5,000 pounds of tobacco - 100 acres, part of "Mount Hope." Henry and Anne his wife (she being first privately examined) acknowledged before Robert Norrest Wright and John Earle. Alienation fine, two shillings sterling.

514. 24 March 1742 N. Wright and Edward Godwin, appointed by Robert Norrest Wright to view and value 227 acres called "Thomas'es Addition," lying in Tully's Neck - the right of Tilden Thomas, a minor under the care of John Clothier, his guardian - find one log'd house, 20 x 16 feet, new; one log'd house, 16 x 18 feet, new; one old small clapboard dwelling house; one old small log'd dwelling house; one old small log'd corn house, not worth repairing; one old 40 foot tobacco house, much out of repair; about 120 bearing apple trees and some other fruit trees; the fencing in middling good repair. The annual value 600 pounds of tobacco, clear of quitrents and repairs; the guardian to clear 30 acres and have use of timber.

515. 24 March 1742 Edward Brown and William Hopper, appointed by Thomas

515. Wilkinson to view and value "Chesterfield" and 70 acres, "Chesterfield Addition;" 200 acres, part of "Neglect;" and 100 acres, "Clayton's Levells" - the right of Edward Clayton, a minor, William Coursey, his guardian - find on "Chesterfield" and "Chesterfield Addition" one dwelling house, part old and part new, 52 x 16 feet with a
12 foot shed (the old part much out of repair); a milk house, part
brick and part clapboard, 26 x 15 in good repair; clapboard kitchen
with a shed and stack of brick chimneys, 40 x 20 feet, very old and
much decayed; a store house with a shed at each end, 25 x 16, out
repair; a log'd quarter with a brick chimney, 20 x 15 feet, out of
repair; a log'd corn house, 15 x 8 feet; a tobacco house, 40 x 20
feet, bastard framed, in good repair; a small young orchard of about
60 apple trees; the ground paled in for a garden, 16 x 70 feet; two
log'd houses, each 20 x 16 feet, very old and much decayed; a
smith's shop, 15 feet square, very old and much decayed; an old
tann house; the fencing reasonable good repair; the annual value,
1,400 pounds of tobacco. On "Neglect," one old dwelling house with
mud chimney, 15 feet square; a corn house, 16 x 8 feet; a tobacco
house, 52 x 22 feet, bastard framed, the cover soon wants repairing; the fencing reasonable good repair; annual value 500 pounds of
tobacco; the guardian not to clear any more ground or down any timber except for tobacco hogsheads and repairs. "Clayton's Levells"
is without improvements and not of value; the guardian can clear 40
acres and cut timber for buildings.

516. 23 December 1742 - 26 March 1743 William Dawson and John Clayland,
appointed by Robert Lloyd to view and value 150 acres, part of
"Trustram," left by Edmund Thomas, deceased, to his son Edmund -
find about 40 acres of cleared land and on the same, part of an old
dwelling house, 15 x 16 feet, scarcely habitable; also a rough built
tobacco house, 30 x 22 feet, about 10 feet pitch, the roof leaky and
some of the posts near rotten off at the bottom and stands in immed-
iate need of repairing and propping; and about 400 rails laying in
a kind of ruinous old broken fence on the western side of the plantation. William Holden, present guardian to Edmund Thomas, is permitted to clear on any part, 12 acres of fresh land for tobacco
ground and the privilege of mauling new rails for the use of the
plantation; the annual value, 150 pounds of tobacco to be paid to
Edmund at full age.

516. 22 March 1742 - 28 March 1743 Richard Bennett, Gentleman, to William Tilghman, Gentleman - in consideration of love and affection
and further payment of five shillings - part of "Poplar Plains" -
lying in the woods at the head of Chester River, originally surveyed for Cornelius Comegys for 500 acres - made over to Bennett by
Charles Hynson of Kent County, Gentleman, to whom it was made over
by Richard Howell of Philadelphia, Gentleman, and Letitia his wife,
one of the daughters of Coll. Edward Scott of Kent County, in trust.
191 acres adjoining a part of the same sold to Matthew Tilghman.
Wits: Thomas Clarke, J. Loockerman, Jr. Acknowledged before Levin
Gale, Justice of the Provincial Court. Alienation fine, seven shillings, eight pence sterling, paid to Richard Tilghman.

517. 31 March 1743 Richard Tilghman, William Tilghman and James Tilghman to Charles, the Lord Proprietary - a Bond of ₤1,000 for the con-
tinuance of Richard Tilghman as Clerk of Queen Ann's County. Wits:
Robert Norrest Wright, Charles Downes. Acknowledged before Thomas
Wilkinson and James Brown. 20 March 1743.

518. 14 July 1742 - 2 April 1743 Gilbert Turner, sometime of Talbot County, now of Carteret County, North Carolina, Planter, to Lewis Trott
of Onslow County, North Carolina, Planter - Power of Attorney to
sell "Hacker's Forrest," 200 acres in Queen Ann's County, on the
west side of Tuckahoe Creek - bequeathed to me by deceased John Rogers, my uncle. Wits: Joseph Watts, Elizabeth Dudley. Proven by
Lewis Trott before John Dudley, Justice of the Peace for Onslow County, 18 July 1742. 7 September 1742 Joseph Watts certified before
Henry Casson.

519. 6 October 1742 - 2 April 1743 Gilbert Turner of Carteret County,
North Carolina and Lewis Trott of Onslow County, to George Baynard -
consideration 3,000 pounds of tobacco - 200 acres, "Hacker's Forrest"
on the west side of Tuckahoe Creek, adjoining "Branford," formerly
laid out for Coll. William Digges - being so much due to John Hacker
of Talbot County by assignment from William Coursey, the assignee
of William Hemsley - being part of a warrant for 620 acres granted
to the said Hemsley, 6 December 1696, as appears by a patent granted
to John Hacker, 10 October 1707. Wits: W. Jumpe, Henry Casson.
Lewis Trott acknowledged the deed 6 October before Henry Casson.
Henry Feddeman witnessed Trott's receipt to George Baynard.

521. 14 April 1743 - 28 April 1743 Joseph Mangarage to John Hart - two
cows and two heiffers; eight ewes and lambs at James Hutchins' upon
William Coburn's plantation and all rights to my personal estate for
value received. Wits: Thomas Wilkinson, Christopher Wilkinson.
Acknowledged before Thomas Wilkinson.

521. 11 April 1743 - 28 April 1743 Richard Wells, Planter, to Richard
Wells, Jr. - consideration 2,000 pounds of tobacco - 50 acres, part
of "Bath." Acknowledged before James Brown and Humphery Wells, Jr.
Alienation fine, two shillings sterling, paid to Richard Tilghman.

522. 11 April 1743 - 28 April 1743 Richard Wells to Zorababel Wells -
consideration 2,500 pounds of tobacco - 50 acres, part of "Bath's
Addition." Acknowledged before James Brown and Humphery Wells, Jr.
Alienation fine, two shillings sterling.

523. 27 April 1743 - 28 April 1743 James Robass, Millwright, to Daniel
Cheston of Chester Town - consideration ₤152.8.0 current money -
20 acres of land, granted to Robass for building a watermill on the
Red Lyon Branch - parts of two tracts, one is "London;" two is
"Crompton," each containing 10 acres - and the watermill on the land
with all the wheels, stones, tackle, apparell, furniture, utensils,
appurtenances and also one single millstone on the premises now lying - for the residue of the term (of lease). Wits: James Calder,

523. James Nicols. Acknowledged before S. Knight.

525. 4 May 1743 Christopher Wilkinson to Richard Tilghman - in consideration of ₤77 current money - mortgages one walnut desk; six trunks; three chests; twelve large silver spoons; six teaspoons and tongs; one cane couch; all my potts and the tobacco crop, corn, wheat, oats and beans growing on the plantation I now live on, on the land called "Royston," with all of my personal estate - due before 1 October 1743. Wits: Thomas Wilkinson, John Tilden, Jr. Acknowledged before Thomas Wilkinson.

525. 21 April 1743 - 5 May 1743 Thomas Betton, Planter, to Arthur Emory, Gentleman - consideration ₤25 sterling - 40 acres, part of "Fortune" near the branches of Coursey's Creek - adjoining "Bristol Marsh." Acknowledged to Thomas Wilkinson and Joseph Sudler. Alienation fine one shilling, seven pence sterling, paid to Richard Tilghman.

527. 14 May 1743 Thomas Reed, Jr., Master of the ship "Polly," at anchor in Wye River and bound from thence for London, will take tobacco on freight at ₤9 sterling per tonn, consigned to Mr. Samuel Hyde, Merchant.

527. 22 February 1742 - 19 May 1743 William Fishbourn of Philadelphia, son and heir of William Fishbourn, deceased, and Jane Fishbourn, the widow and relict of William (dec'd), to Jacob Loockerman of Talbot County, Planter - consideration ₤12 money of Pensilvania paid to his father - 213 acres, part of "Providence," originally surveyed for Andrew Skinner, Samuel Winslow and Henry Parker - lying on the east side of the southwest branch of Corsica Creek - adjoining a part belonging to Thomas Wilkinson. Power of Attorney given to John Loockerman and John Welsh. Wits: John Frazier, Silas Prior, Peter David. John Frazier acknowledged to Robert Norrest Wright and Thomas Wilkinson. Alienation fine, eight shillings, six pence, half penny sterling, paid to Richard Tilghman.

529. 17 May 1743 - 19 May 1743 Sophia Abrahams and Jacob Abrahams to Joseph Newnam - consideration ₤35 and 1,600 pounds of tobacco - 150 acres, part of "Devinishes' Chance," on the west side of Unicorne Branch - adjoining a parcel of land laid out for Francis Shepherd called "Shepherd's Fold," containing 500 acres - the 150 acres conveyed is the dwelling plantation of Jeremiah Thomas, deceased. Acknowledged before James Brown and Humphery Wells, Jr. Alienation fine, six shillings sterling.

530. 27 May 1743 Matthew Tilghman of Talbot County, to Richard Tilghman - consideration five shillings sterling - 100 acres called the "Adventure," originally taken up by John Morgan, on the north side of Read's Creek. Matthew and Anne his wife, acknowledged before Robert Norrest Wright and Robert Lloyd.

531. 10 June 1743 George Baynard to Michael Hussey and Margret his wife - leases 60 acres, part of "Hacker's Forrest," adjoining "Branford" -

531. from 1 January last for a term of fourteen years. George Baynard
      to build a log dwelling house, 20 x 15 feet and one tobacco house,
      30 x 20 feet with a 10 foot pitch by next Fall - Michael Hussey to
      find the carpenter that builds the tobacco house and accomodations
      (i.e. food and lodging) - Baynard, within three years, to find 100
      apple trees and help plant them, Michael to keep them within a fence
      so they cannot be damaged by creatures; and to have timber for use
      of the plantation. Acknowledged before William Jumpe and Henry Cas-
      son.

532. 30 May 1743 - 13 June 1743 John Lee, Planter, to John Nevill, Plan-
      ter - consideration 3,500 pounds of tobacco - 50 acres called "Solo-
      mon's Outlet," lying on the west side of Red Lyon Branch near the
      head of the Horsepen Branch and on the south side of "Camberwell."
      Part of a warrant for 200 acres granted to Daniel Sherwood of Tal-
      bot County, 7 July 1740 and assigned to John Lee, 18 September 1740.
      Acknowledged before James Brown and Humphery Wells, Jr. Alienation
      fine, two shillings sterling, paid to Richard Tilghman.

533. 8 January 1742 - 23 June 1743 Thomas Seward and Rebecca his wife,
      and William Bishop and Anne his wife to William Clayton, Gentleman -
      consideration 16,000 pounds of tobacco - 400 acres called "Bishop's
      Fields," formerly lying in Talbot County. Thomas, Rebecca and Wil-
      liam acknowledged their deed before Thomas Wilkinson and James Brown
      (Rebecca having been first privately examined). Alienation fine,
      eight shillings, sterling.

534. 9 June 1743 - 23 June 1743 Elizabeth Hawkins, Widow and relict of
      Coll. Ernault Hawkins, to Richard Bennett, Merchant - consideration
      Ŀ20 sterling - a tract of land called "Stratton," patented to Coll.
      Hawkins for 1,000 acres. Wits: Thomas Wilkinson, Henry Casson,
      Charles Browne. Acknowledged to Wilkinson and Casson. Alienation
      fine, forty shillings sterling.

535. 9 June 1743 - 28 June 1743 James Davis of Sussex County upon Dela-
      ware, Plaisterer, brother and heir at law to Sybila Beckett, lately
      Wilkinson als Sybila Davis late of Sussex County, to Jeremiah Gres-
      ingham of Talbot County, Planter. "John Davis, late of Talbot Coun-
      ty, father of Sybila, by his will dated 18 December 1712, devised to
      her and his daughters Frances and Elizabeth, part of "Davis'es
      Range" - on 2 December 1729, William Elbert, Joyner, of Talbot, and
      the said Frances, then his wife, and Sybila Wilkinson, Widow, and
      Elizabeth Davis made a division of the said tract." Now James Davis,
      in consideration of 7,000 pounds of tobacco and one riding cart, con-
      veys all of Sybilla's part of "Davis'es Range." Acknowledged to
      Thomas Wilkinson and Henry Casson. Alienation fine, eight shillings
      sterling.

537. 28 June 1743 John Emory and Anne his wife, to Thomas Lee, Planter -
      consideration 12,000 pounds of tobacco - 100 acres, part of "Hawkin-
      ses Pharsalia" - lying on the west side of the tract above the rid-
      ing over of Beaverdam Branch and about 50 perches below the dwelling

537. house that William Emory formerly lived in - and adjoining "Stratton." John and Anne (she being first privately examined) acknowledged before Humphery Wells, Jr. and Henry Casson. Alienation fine, four shillings sterling paid to Richard Tilghman.

538. Recorded 28 June 1743. City and County of Exon (Great Britain) - at the General Quarter Sessions held in the Guildhall, 12 July last, before William Newcombe, Esquire, Mayor; Nathaniel Dowdney; Thomas Coplestone; Emanuel Hale; William Habbath; John Newcombe and Matthew Spry, Aldermen and Justices of the Peace - Mary, wife of Samuel Merry, Dyer, was convicted of stealing two brass cocks, valued at ten pence, also a silver hafted knife and fork, valued at ten pence, the property of William Bryant. Liable for a whipping as punishment, her sentence commuted to transportation to one of His Majestie's colonies in America for a term of seven years; Dowdney and Newcombe to contract for the same. John Gandy, Clerk of the Peace.

William Dowdney, convicted of felony 5 October last, sentenced to be sent to the colonies for seven years; Richard Beavis, William Clifford Martyn, Esquires, Justices of the Peace, appointed to make the contract, which was given to George Buck, County Devon, Merchant, who agreed to transport them within three months of date, 8 November 1742. John Fortescue and Isaac Truslade, witnessed for William C. Martyn; William Strange and John Laskey for George Buck, who made the contract over to Capt. John Bissick, Commander of the ship "Kent," at Biddeford, 3 December 1742. Wits: John Wurton, John Every.

539. At the Sessions of Goal Delivery held at the Castle of Exon, County Devon, 29 March last, Amos Harding, Simon Baily, John Southwood, Lawrence Wheeler, George Corkrane, John Gale, John Staddon als Stanton, Richard Hooper, Daniel Spurway, Stephen Taylor, William Kerslake, Bartholomew Croot, William Drewy, Richard Hollier and Ann Dodd, were convicted of felonies and sentenced to be taken to the colonies for terms of fourteen years. Sir Henry Northcotte, Robert Stuckey, William Clifford Martyn, Richard Beavis, Caleb Juglett, George Southcott, William Tucker and Thomas Ball, Justices of the Peace (or any two of them) were appointed to contract for their transportation. Beavis and Martyn agreed with George Buck of Bideford for this service, 8 November 1742. Witnesses, Joseph Hasse, Isaac Truslade.

540. City and County of Exon, 20 September last - before William Newcombe, Mayor; John Belfield, Sergeant at Law and Records; Nathaniel Dowdney; Thomas Copplestone; Emanuel Hale and John Newcombe, Aldermen and Justices of the Peace - Susanna Jeffrey of Exon, single, was convicted of stealing a thread purse, valued at one penny and five guineas. Liable to punishment of burning in the hand, she was sentence to be taken to the colonies for a period of seven years. John Gandy, Clerk. George Buck assigned this contract to Captain John Bissick, Commander of the ship "Kent," 3 December 1742.

50.

QUEEN ANNE COUNTY LAND RECORDS - R. T. C 1743 - 1751

Page
001. 25 February 1742 - 25 July 1743 Thomas Bostock to Thomas Davis -
consideration 2,400 pounds of tobacco - 50 acres called the "Hollow
Flat" - lying on the east side of Beaver Dam Branch below Tom Jones'
Pond. Acknowledged before James Downes and Henry Casson.

002. 22 March 1742 - 25 July 1743 James Ponder, Planter, to his son Rich-
ard Ponder - a gift of love and affection - 75 acres, part of "Clouds'
Adventure" - where James Ponder lives upon. Acknowledged before
James Brown and D. Thompson.

002. 1 July 1743 NOTICE: Thomas Reed, Master of the ship, "Mary," now
riding at anchor in Wye River, bound for London - will take tobacco
on board at ₤9 sterling per tonn, consigned to James Buchanan, Merchant.

002. 26 July 1743 William Kirkham, late of Queen Ann's County, Planter,
and Mary his wife, to Samuel Dickinson of Kent County on Delaware,
Province of Pennsylvania, Gentleman - consideration ₤75 current money - 175 acres called "Youghall," formerly in Talbot now in Queen
Ann's County, north side of Choptank River, adjoining "Tuttlefields,"
formerly laid out for John Ingram - also 200 acres, "Tuttlefields."
Wits: Nathaniel Knotts, Charles Goldsborough. William and Mary (she
being first privately examined) acknowledged their deed before Edward
Tilghman and William Hopper.

004. 11 July 1743 - 26 July 1743 John Hollingsworth, Planter, to Richard
Porter, Jr., Chirurgeon - consideration ₤175 paid and mortgage given
14 January last and further consideration of ₤40 - Hollingsworth's
dwelling plantation, part of "Annthrop," the remainder after the sale
to William Campbell. John and Elizabeth his wife (she being first
privately examined) acknowledged before Robert Norrest Wright and
James Brown.

006. 6 May 1743 - 26 July 1743 John Andrews, Planter, and Hannah his wife,
and Benjamin Newmam and Hannah his wife, to John Maccoy and James
Maccoy, Shumakers - consideration 6,000 pounds of tobacco - 118½
acres of land, part of "Smith's Delight" - on the Red Lyon Branch to
the east of Richard Ponder and Sarah his wife - as by a deed of par-
tition made between Ezekial Hamer and Richard and Sarah Ponder,
11 September 1727. John and Hannah (she being first privately examined) acknowledged before James Brown and Humphrey WElls, Jr. Alienation fine, four shillings, nine pence sterling paid to Richard Tilghman. [NOTE: The name "Maccoy" was also written "McCoye" in this same
document.]

007. 21 July 1743 Robert Fowler, Planter, to Richard Tilghman, Gentleman -
consideration ₤31.10.0 current - mortgages part of "Shrewsbury," 150
acres of land whereon he (Fowler) now dwells - payment due on or before 10 November 1747. Wits: Robert Lloyd, William Tilghman.

008. 21 July 1743 John Alley, Planter, to Richard Tilghman, Gentleman -
      consideration £64.9.0 current money - mortgages his dwelling planta-
      tion, part of "Adventure" and part of "Confusion" - payment due on
      or before 10 November 1747. Acknowledged before Robert Lloyd and
      William Tilghman.

010. 20 April 1743 - 24 August 1743 John Dempster to David Mills of Dor-
      chester County, Cooper and Carpenter - consideration £5 current -
      Lot Number Seven in Kingstown on Chester River. Acknowledged before
      James Brown and John Earle.

011. 4 May 1743 - 24 August 1743 James Croney of Dorchester County, Plan-
      ter, to John Croney of Queen Ann's County, Planter - consideration
      2,300 pounds of tobacco - 75 acres, part of "Coldraym," formerly laid
      out for John Pitt of Talbot County - lying on Tuckahoe Creek and ad-
      joining "Partnership," formerly laid out for John Pitt and Captain
      Philemon Lloyd. Wits: J. Loockerman, Andrew Jordan.

      James Croney to William Banckes - Power of Attorney, proved at Queens-
      town before Robert Norrest Wright and his Associates by the witnesses
      Loockerman and Jordan. Acknowledged before Robert N. Wright and As-
      sociates by William Banckes.

012. 26 August 1743 John Ayler, Taylor, to Charles Bradley, Planter -
      consideration 2,500 pounds of tobacco - 50 acres, part of "Ayler's
      Hope" - on the east side of Tuckahoe Creek opposite "Dawson's Neck."
      Acknowledged before James Brown and Joseph Sudler. Alienation fine,
      two shillings sterling, paid to Richard Tilghman.

013. 20 April 1743 - 27 August 1743 John Dempster to Thomas Hynson Wright -
      consideration £20 current - Lots Number One and Twenty-seven in Kings-
      towne and also a piece of land lying between Lot Number Two and the
      Chester River. Acknowledged before James Brown and John Earle.

015. 5 September 1743 - 8 September 1743 Margaret Bussells, Spinster, to
      John Comegys, Planter - consideration 3,000 pounds of tobacco - one
      brown cow and yearling; one brown pide cow and yearling; one black
      cow and brindle yearling; one white mare; one black mare; two feather-
      beds with rugg and two blanketts to each with stedds. Wits: Richard
      Wells, Jr., Henry Rochester.

015. 14 March 1742 - 9 September 1743 Richard Powel, Taylor, son and heir
      at law of Elizabeth Norrest, daughter and one of the devisees of Rob-
      ert Norrest, late of Kent County (Maryland) and Mary his wife, to
      Robert Norrest Wright, oldest son and heir at law of Katherine Nor-
      rest, eldest daughter and devisee of Robert Norrest, deceased - con-
      sideration £4 sterling and £5 current money and 7,000 pounds of to-
      bacco - all claim to the lands of Robert Norrest except 50 acres,
      part of "Jones's Park." Richard and Mary (she being first privately
      examined out of his hearing) acknowledged before Charles Downes and
      Thomas Wilkinson.

52.

017. 23 August 1743 - 15 September 1743 Thomas Lee and Frances his wife,
to Timothy Webb - consideration 6,000 pounds of tobacco - 50 acres
called "Watson's Lott," lying in the Long Neck on the east side of
a great swamp issuing out of ye Beaver Dam Marsh. Thomas and Frances (she being first privately examined) acknowledged before James
Brown and Humphery Wells, Jr.

018. 6 May 1742 - 24 October 1743 Robert Gilpin of Whitehaven, County
Cumberland (Eng.), Merchant, to Thomas Bozman of Talbot County,
America, and Tubman Rumball of Whitehaven, Merchant - Power of Attor-
ney to call to account Henry Casson, Merchant, his factor and agent -
to settle accounts due; to collect all money or effects in his hands
or in the hands of any servants under him employed. Wits: William
Barker, Isaac Edgar - who certified the instrument before William
Jumpe.

018. 24 October 1743 Robert Crump to Richard Wells, Jr. - consideration
5,000 pounds of tobacco - 220 acres called "Crumpton," on the west
side of Red Lyon Branch - adjoining "Newport," belonging to Cornelius Comegys. Acknowledged before James Brown and Humphery Wells,
Jr. Alienation fine, eight shillings, ten pence sterling, paid to
Richard Tilghman.

019. Recorded 22 November 1743. "I hereby certifye that James Notts, a
private Continell (sic!) in Captain John Millbourn's Company in the
First Battalion of Coll. Gooch's Regiment, hath served ye Crown of
Great Britain upwards of two years faithfully and is now discharged
from His Majesty's service this 15th day of January 1743/3. Given
under my hand in Hampton, Virginia. Lawrence Washington, Andrew
McKittrick, James Mitchell."

019. 22 November 1743 Thomas Wyatt and Mary Ann his wife, to Henry Wilkinson - consideration 4,000 pounds of tobacco - 50 acres, "Watson's
Chance" - in the Long Neck, west side of Maple Swamp. Acknowledged
before James Brown and Humphery Wells, Jr. Alienation fine, two
shillings sterling, paid to Richard Tilghman.

020. 22 November 1743 William Wyatt and Susannah his wife, to Henry Wilkinson - consideration 3,000 pounds of tobacco - 50 acres, "Wyatt's
Folly" - on the east side of a swamp at the upper end of the Horse-
pen Ridge. William and Susannah (she being first privately examined) acknowledged before James Brown and Humphery Wells, Jr. Alienation fine, two shillings sterling.

021. 23 November 1743 Recorded. Joseph Arrington, guardian to Charles
Seth, a minor, makes petition for evaluation of the orphan's land.
21 September 1743 William Campbell and John Clayland, sworn by Robert Lloyd, viewed an estate of 139½ acres, part of "Mt. Mill, Addition and Bennett's Outlet," with the plantations and improvements
thereon, and found one old dwelling house 50 x 20 feet with one brick
gable end and chimney, very much out of repair; one old dwelling in
the shape of an "L," one part 30 x 17 feet with a stack of brick

021. chimneys in the middle, in good repair; the other part 25 x 15 feet
in middling good repair; one brick milk house, 14 x 8 feet; one old
meat house, 11 x 10 feet, much out of repair; one old logged cornhouse, 14 x 6 feet in reasonable repair; one old 30 x 20 feet tobacco house, very much out of repair; one old 40 x 15 feet tobacco house
very much out of repair and a small old orchard belonging to the dwelling plantation and about 100 acres of cleared ground under reasonable good fencing; and upon the plantation where Thomas Johnings lately dwelt, one old dwelling house, 25 x 15 feet; one small logged dwelling house 15 x 12 feet and one old logg'd corn house, all very mean
except the logg'd dwelling; and about 50 acres of cleared ground under reasonable fencing. The annual value of both places, 1,600
pounds of tobacco clear of quitrents and necessary repairs. The guardian permitted to cut timber for necessary uses and to clear six
acres of land.

022. 22 November 1743 John Dempster to Henry Cully of Kingstown - con-
sideration ₤10 current - Lots Number Twenty-four and Twenty-five in
Kingstown. Acknowledged before James Brown and Humphery Wells, Jr.
Alienation fine, one pence, half pence sterling, paid to R. Tilghman.

022. 23 November 1743 John Coursey to John Seegar, Mariner - consideration ₤30 current money - lease of 200 acres, part of "Coursey's
Range," lately in possession of Charles Annis - near Wallis's Branch
of Wye River, for a term of seven years. Seegar to build a tobacco
house, 40 x 20 feet, covered with clapboards and all further buildings and fences he may think necessary. Acknowledged before James
Brown and Humphery Wells, Jr.

024. 22 October 1743 - 23 November 1743 Richard Bennett to Francis Rochester - in consideration of a competent sum of tobacco - all of his
right by purchase from William Walker of Talbot County, eldest son
and heir of Daniel Walker of Talbot County, to the tract of land
called "Winchester," originally surveyed for Henry Parker for 200
acres which Parker willed to Daniel Walker. Acknowledged before Benjamin Young, Jr., a Justice of the Provincial Court. Alienation fine,
eight shillings sterling.

024. 24 November 1743 Thomas Norman, Taylor, and Sarah his wife, to Benjamin Toulson, Planter - consideration ₤6 current money and one stear -
30 acres on Kent Island, part of "Copedges Range." Thomas and Sarah
(she being first privately examined) acknowledged before James Brown
and Joseph Sudler. Alienation fine, one shilling, three pence sterling.

026. 25 November 1743 - 26 November 1743 George Prouse, Planter, and Jane
his wife, of Talbot County, to Richard Chance, Planter - in consideration of 157 acres near the head of Tredhaven Creek in Talbot County,
part of "Cumberland" and part of "Chance Help," conveyed by Richard
and Eleanor his wife - 200 acres called "Bear Point," on the northeast branch of Choptank River - adjoining the land laid out for John
Ingram. Wits: Nicholas Glen, John Plummer. George and Jane (she

54.

026. being first privately examined out of his hearing) acknowledged their
deed before Robert Norrest Wright and his Associate Justices. Alienation fine, four shillings sterling, paid to Richard Tilghman.

027. 30 July 1743 - 6 November 1743 John Ruth, Planter, to Thomas Baly,
Jr., son of Jacob Baly, deceased - consideration 500 pounds of tobacco - 6 acres of land, part of "Larrington," on the Southwest Branch
of Island Creek - beginning at the bounded tree of the land Jacob
Bayly bought of William Bishop called "Bishop's Outlett." Wits:
Charles Downes and John Brown, before whom John Ruth made his acknow-
ledgment. Alienation fine, three pence sterling.

028. 24 November 1743 - 26 November 1743 John Sinnett, Carpenter, to
Thomas Shobruks, Planter - consideration 3,000 pounds of tobacco -
100 acres, all of "Wellen," lying in the woods between the Southeast
and Southwest Branches of Island Creek. Acknowledged before James
Brown and Joseph Sudler. Alienation fine, four shillings sterling.

029. 24 December 1743 - 5 January 1743 John Nabb to John Brown - consideration 4,000 pounds of tobacco - 100 acres, part of "Marshy Creek"
on the east side of Tuckahoe Creek, near Lowe's Marsh. Acknowledged
before Robert Norrest WRight and William Hopper. Alienation fine,
four shillings sterling.

030. 12 September 1743 - 5 February 1743 Thomas Bullen to Mary Knowles,
now wife of Jonathon Nicols of Queen Ann's County - reference to the
will of John Knowles who left all of his estate, real and personal,
to his two daughters, Margaret and Mary Knowles, with reversion to
his brother, Thomas Bullen, if either should die without lawful issue; Margaret Knowles having since died in her minority and her part
of John's estate became the property of Thomas Bullen. In consideration of the lofe and affection he (Thomas) bears, conveys all of his
rights to the real and personal estate of John Knowles except for one
negro slave called "Jemmy the younger," now in his possession. Wits:
Susannah Kendrick, Edward Legg. Acknowledged before Henry Hooper,
Justice of the Provincial Court.

031. 21 January 1743 - 6 February 1743 Daniel Bridges Paxton, Planter, to
William Durding, Planter - consideration 2,500 pounds of tobacco -
50 acres, part of "Powell's Fancy," lying at the head of Wye River
Branch - adjoining "Batchelor's Chance," in the possession of John
Emory. Wits: John Emory, Vall. Green. Acknowledged before William
Tilghman and Edward Tilghman, Justices of the Peace. Alienation
fine, two shillings sterling, paid to Richard Tilghman.

032. 6 March 1743 Thomas Wilkinson, Gentleman, to Thomas Hynson Wright -
consideration 15,000 pounds of tobacco - a mulatto girl called "Anne,"
about seventeen years to serve; seven old featherbeds and furniture;
one old mare called "Chess"; one young bay mare called "Chess;" one
old bay horse called "Duke;" one young bay horse called "Prince;"

032. one grey mare called "Fancy;" one bay mare called "Fancy;" one small
black horse called "Mink" or "Dover;" one old bay mare called "Trip;"
nine sows; seven young cattle; eighteen head of sheep; 5 small old
tables; four small old chests; twelve old chaires; one servant man
named William Evans about four years to serve. Wits: Charles Downes,
John Chaires. Acknowledged before Charles Downes.

033. 8 December 1743 - 9 February 1743 James Paul Heath of Cecil County,
Merchant, to Samuel McCosh, Planter - consideration ₤80 money of the
Province - two parcels of land on the east side of the Southwest
Branch of Island Creek - one is part of "Upper Heathworth," about
88 acres; the other is part of "Collins' Refusall" - adjoining the
first, about 112 acres. Wits: John Baldwin, Pereg. Ward, Justices
of the Peace for Cecil County. James Paul Heath and Rebecca his wife
acknowledged before them, Rebecca having been previously examined
out of hearing of her husband. Certified by William Knight, Clerk
of Cecil County Court. Alienation fine, eight shillings sterling,
paid to Richard Tilghman.

034. 10 January 1743 - 9 February 1743 Peter Cummerford of Talbot County,
Gentleman, to Thomas Marsh, Gentleman - consideration ₤200 sterling
money of Great Britain - 200 acres called "Neglect" on Kent Island -
adjoining the land of Dennis Brinn's and Thomas Marsh's land called
"Cabin Neck," on Tarkill Creek. Wits: W. Thomas, John Goldsborough.
Robert Harwood and James Porter witnessed Cummerford's receipt to
Thomas Marsh. Acknowledged in Talbot County Court before Thomas and
Goldsborough, who were certified by John Leeds, Clerk.

035. 15 December 1743 - 16 February 1743 Thomas Thomas and Susannah his
wife, to Oneale Price - consideration 1,000 pounds of tobacco and
₤2.5.0 current money - 11 acres of land, part of "Winfield" - in
Tully's Neck - adjoining the land of Charles Oneale sold to William
Satterfield. Thomas and Susannah (she being first privately examined) acknowledged their deed before Robert Norrest Wright and William Hopper. Alienation fine, five pence half penny sterling.

036. 8 March 1743 Thomas Hynson Wright, Gentleman, to Nathaniel Read -
in consideration of an exchange of 100 acres of land where Nathaniel
dwelleth, part of "New Reading" - gives 300 acres, part of "Tom's
Fancy Enlarged" - in Tully's Neck, adjoining "Smith's Forrest," com-
monly known as "Smith's Mannor." Acknowledged before Robert Norrest
Wright and Robert Lloyd. Alienation fine, twelve shillings sterling.

037. 8 March 1743 Thomas Hynson Wright to Sarah, wife of Nathaniel Read -
consideration 3,000 pounds of tobacco - 100 acres, part of "Tom's
Fancy Enlarged" - adjoining a former purchase. Acknowledged before
R. N. Wright and Robert Lloyd. Alienation fine, four shillings sterling.

038. 29 March 1744 Robert Basnett, Carpenter, to Thomas Marsh, Gentleman -
consideration 4,994 pounds of tobacco - a servant man named Stephen
Moray, about five years to serve; two cows and calves; two cows bigg

56.

038. with calf; twenty head of hoggs, some large, some small; one bay
gelding; one bay mare; two featherbeds; two ruggs and two blanketts;
a mortgage due on or before 10 June next. Wits: John Hawkins and
William Goldsborough. Acknowledged before Charles Downes.

038. 20 March 1743 - 28 March 1744 John Baker, Laborer, to Nicholas
Glen - consideration 1,965 pounds of tobacco and 1,178 pounds of tobacco due from me to Charles Browne & Company paid by Nicholas Glen,
and 756 pounds of tobacco due from me to Thomas Hynson Wright, Sheriff, paid by N. Glen - sells 15 barrells of Indian corn in a house
at Mrs. Alice Lloyd's Quarter; my share of the crop of tobacco made
by me with the hands of Mrs. Lloyd last year; the whole being divided in six shares and a half; nine pewter plates and three pewter
dishes; two chests; two rush bottomed chairs; one iron pott; one
frying pan; one old bed and bedding; one man's saddle; two pails and
a piggin; one New England bucket; one broadcloth coat, vest and
breeches of a lightish colour - all put in the possession of Nicholas
Glen by the delivery of one silk handkerchief. Wits: T. H. Wright,
N. S. Wright. Acknowledged before William Hopper.

039. 22 November 1743 - 29 March 1744 Francis Rochester, Innholder, to
John Foreacres - consideration 7,000 pounds of tobacco - 100 acres,
part of 300 acres called "Tully's Lott" - sold by Darby Oryan before
his death, to John Foreacres - Francis Rochester, his executor.
Acknowledged before James Brown and Humphery Wells, Jr. Alienation
fine, four shillings sterling paid to Richard Tilghman.

040. 22 March 1743 - 30 March 1744 Coll. George Gale of Somerset County,
Province of Maryland, to Archibald Jackson, Planter - consideration
£30 current money - his claim to 300 acres of land, part of "Ratcliffe" - adjoining "Old Town" and the land of William Hewbanks.
This is part of the land of Samuel Groom, Jr., two tracts called
"Partnership" and "Ratcliffe," containing 1,000 acres each; formerly
granted to Samuel Groom the elder - lying in the freshes of Great
Choptank River. Sold by James Hollyday and Henry Hooper, trustees
appointed to sell the land of Samuel Groom, Jr. to satisfy a mortgage of £820.5.7 given to Levin Denwood of Somerset County, deceased,
Betty and Levin Gale, his executors, 20 September 1733. George and
John Gale purchased the land at public sale - John Gale is since
dead. Wits: John Williams, Levin Dashiell. Acknowledged in Somerset
County Court before William Stoughten and Associates. Thomas Hayward, Clerk of Somerset County. Alienation fine, twelve shillings
sterling, paid to Richard Tilghman.

041. 21 March 1743 - 30 March 1744 Philip Davis of Kent County (Md.),
Planter, to Charles and Solomon Clayton, the sons of Solomon Clayton, deceased - consideration 13,000 pounds of tobacco, paid by
Solomon (deceased) in his lifetime - conveyed to Charles at age twenty one and to his brother Solomon if Charles should die without lawful issue - the land called "Mt. Maluck," 150 acres lying on the west
side of Andover Branch. Wits: Ebenez. Blackiston and Thomas Hynson,
before whom Philip and Elizabeth his wife acknowledged (she being

041. first privately examined). Certified by John Smith, Clerk of Kent
      County. William Coursey, for Charles and Solomon Clayton, paid six
      shillings sterling for the alienation fine, to Richard Tilghman.

042. 21 December 1743 - 31 March 1744 Henry Casson, Gentleman, to John
      Baynard, Gentleman, Gentleman - sells his interest in twenty acres
      of land with a mill thereon, on the east side of Tuckahoe Creek -
      granted to them in 1739 for a term of eighty years, paying yearly
      the sum of ten shillings to Eleanor Anthony, Rebecca Leonard, Mar-
      garet Knowles and Mary Knowles, from whom the land was taken. Henry
      Casson and Esther his wife, acknowledged before Robert Norrest Wright
      and William Hopper.

044. 31 March 1744 Joseph Tryal, Planter, to John Jackson, Phisician -
      consideration 20,000 pounds of tobacco - 100 acres of land, part of
      "Smithfield" - given by John Simmonds and Mary his wife to Joseph
      Tryal, father of Joseph the grantor - also 38 acres, part of "Hitt
      or Miss," conveyed by Thomas and Elizabeth Wilkinson to Joseph Try-
      al, 29 June 1737. Joseph and Sarah his wife (she being first pri-
      vately examined out of his hearing) acknowledged before Robert Lloyd
      and James Brown. Alienation fine, five shillings sterling.

045. 5 April 1744 Jacob Loockerman of Talbot County to John Jackson,
      Phisician - consideration ₤90 current money and 7,500 pounds of to-
      bacco - 213 acres, part of "Providence," lying on the east side of
      the Southwest Branch of Coursica Creek - purchased of William Fish-
      bourne and Jane Fishbourne of the City of Philadelphia, 22 February
      1742. Jacob and Elizabeth his wife (she being first privately exam-
      ined) acknowledged before Robert Lloyd and William Tilghman. Alien-
      ation fine, four shillings, three pence sterling.

046. 31 January 1743 - 5 April 1744 Daniel Bridges Paxton, Planter, to
      John Emory, Planter - in exchange of 90 acres of land near the Horse-
      head on the west side of Choptank River Branch, some distance from
      the branch, and further consideration of 172½ pounds of tobacco and
      twelve shillings current money - gives quit claim to land called
      "Powell's Fancy" - adjoining the lands of William Durding; "Russeth;"
      "Prowses Park" and "Ditteridge," containing 90 acres. Wits: Vall.
      Green, John Burnett. Acknowledged before James Brown and Joseph
      Sudler. Alienation fine, three shillings, seven pence sterling.

048. 5 April 1744 - 10 April 1744 William Simpson and Mary his wife, to
      Thomas Hynson Wright - consideration 8,000 pounds of tobacco - 100
      acres, part of "Larrington," on the Southwest branch of Island Creek.
      Wits: John Coursey, Richard Holding. William and Mary acknowledged
      their deed (she being first privately examined out of his hearing)
      before Robert Lloyd and William Tilghman.

049. 26 April 1744 Jeremiah Gresingham of Talbot County, Planter, to
      William Campbell, Planter - consideration 9,000 pounds of tobacco -
      185 acres, part of "Davis's Range" - adjoining "Smith's Forrest,"
      part of a purchase from James Davis, heir at law to his sister, Sy-

049. billa Beckett, lately Sybilla Wilkinson. Wits: James Tilghman, Christopher Thomas. Acknowledged before Robert Lloyd and William Tilghman. Alienation fine, seven shillings five pence sterling, paid to Richard Tilghman.

050. 29 March 1744 - 17 May 1744 John Dempster, Planter, to Thomas Marsh, Gentleman - consideration 1,400 pounds of tobacco - Lots Number Four and Five in Kings Town. Wits: Robert Lloyd, James Brown.

052. 11 May 1744 - 17 May 1744 Thomas Awbrey of Fairfax County, Colony of Virginia, Planter, to Christopher Cox, Planter - consideration ₤59 sterling - 179 acres, part of "Prophecy," on the southwest branch of Island Creek adjoining "Waterford," laid out for Andrew Skinner and Nathaniel Evitt and "Readbourne," in the possession of James Holly- day - heretofore sold by William Marsh to James Earle, deceased; and also another parcel of "Prophecy," part of 100 acres sold to James Earle by Richard Cole, 38 acres - all of "Heath's Discovery," 23 acres adjoining "Larrington," taken up by John Broadribb and convey- ed to James Earle by James Paul Heath. Wits: George Stewart, James Calder. Acknowledged before Robert Gordon, Justice of the Provincial Court. Alienation fine, five shillings, three pence, half penny ster- ling.

053. 3 May 1744 - 24 May 1744 Ann Dayley, Widow, to Edmond Kelly, Coop- er - in consideration of love and affection and five shillings paid by Kelly - 50 acres, part of "Isaac's Chance," adjoining the land of Philip Conner on Kent Island. Acknowledged before William Tilghman and Edward Tilghman. Alienation fine, two shillings sterling.

054. 16 December 1743 - 14 June 1744 Anne King of Kent County, Pennsyl- vania, to Samuel Swift, Planter - consideration 2,500 pounds of to- bacco - 50 acres called "Foster's Folly," on the west side of the main branch of the Choptank River - on a small branch called Indian Poll Branch. Acknowledged before James Brown and Humphery Wells, Jr.

055. 7 June 1744 - 14 June 1744 Christopher Wilkinson to Sweatnam Burn, only son and heir of Hannah Burn, eldest daughter of John Sweatnam, deceased, eldest son of Richard Sweatnam of Talbot County, deceased - consideration 7,000 pounds of tobacco paid by Matthew Dockery - part of "Royston," according to a deed made by Edward Burn and Hannah his wife, father and mother of Sweatnam Burn, to Christopher Wilkinson, deceased, father of Christopher Wilkinson, grantor, for 475 acres. Acknowledged before William and Edward Tilghman. Alienation fine, nine shillings, six pence sterling, paid by Matthew Dockery.

056. 17 May 1744 - 14 June 1744 Elizabeth Hawkins, Gentlewoman, to Am- brose Wright, Planter - consideration 3,067 pounds of tobacco - 46 acres, part of a 638 acre resurvey called "Hawkins Farm" - on Cour- sica Creek. Acknowledged before Edward Tilghman and William Hopper. Alienation fine, one shilling, ten pence sterling.

057. 12 July 1744 "Shipped by Mrs. Elizabeth Hawkins on the ship "Polly,"
      Master Thomas Reed, Jr., bound for London and now at anchor in Wye
      River - four hogsheads of Maryland leaf tobacco to be delivered to
      Mr. Samuel Hyde, Merchant in London - he to pay freight of ₤9 ster-
      ling per tonn. Maryland 19 July 1743. Signed, Thomas Reed, Jr."

058. 6 August 1744 - 16 August 1744 James Robass, Millwright, to Thomas
      Hynson Wright - consideration 9,983 pounds of tobacco - one small old
      schooner called the "Vallentine" with 'anker,' cable and rigging; two
      featherbeds, weight 100 pounds; two ruggs; two blanketts, two sheets;
      two boulsters; two pillows and two bedsteads; one 7-gallon iron pot;
      one 3-gallon iron pot; three pewter dishes; six pewter plates; two
      pewter basons; one small square walnut table; four rushbottomed
      chairs; four new augers; fifteen carpenter's and joyner's chisels and
      gouges; four turner's chisels and gouges; one large laithe screw;
      three handsaws; one broad axe; one carpenter's adze; one new cross-
      cut saw; one handsaw being delivered in the name of the whole. Wits:
      Humphery Wells, Jr., James Phillips. Acknowledged before Humphery
      Wells, Jr.

058. 4 April 1744 - 16 August 1744 John Dempster and Dowdall Thompson,
      appointed by James Brown to view and value the plantation of James
      Butler, a minor; his guardian John Ruth - formerly known as Thomas
      Vanderford's plantation, lying above Collins' Mill and adjoining the
      plantation that John Hayes, Jr. now lives on - about 125 acres -
      70 acres cleared and very little board or shingle timber. On the
      cleared ground is one young bearing orchard of about 70 apple trees;
      a small nursery of young apple trees and a young bearing orchard of
      peach trees with sundry cherry trees and other fruit trees; one old
      hewed logg'd dwelling house about 25 feet long; one old post in the
      ground boarded tobacco house about 30 feet in length and an old 20
      feet round, rough logg'd tobacco house; the fencing is and may be put
      in good repair by the rails already mauled thereon. The yearly rent
      is 800 pounds of tobacco including quitrents. Wit: James Brown.

058. 9 June 1744 - 16 August 1744 Michael Earle, Mariner, heir at law to
      Ann Earle, one sister and coheir of William Carpenter deceased, to
      Richard Tilghman, Gentleman - consideration ₤5 current - about 9
      acres, a moiety of "Carpenter's Outlett," taken up by the said Wil-
      liam Carpenter - adjoining "Tilghman's Hermitage." Acknowledged be-
      fore William and Edward Tilghman.

059. 31 March 1744 - 16 August 1744 Thomas Hynson Wright to John Coursey -
      consideration ₤80 current silver - 223 acres, part of "Hemsley's
      Brittland Rectified," on the west side of Wye River otherwise called
      Morgan's Creek at the head of Matthew Smith's Cove. Lying between
      the dwellings of John Coursey and John Smith, the line runs to Sad-
      dler's Cove and to the place where the beginning tree of "Coursey's
      Range" did formerly stand. Acknowledged before Edward Tilghman and
      William Hopper. Alienation fine, eight shillings, eleven pence ster-
      ling paid to Richard Tilghman.

060. 5 July 1744 - 16 August 1744   Thomas Wilkinson and Elizabeth his
wife, to John Jackson, Gentleman - consideration ₤15.10.0 sterling
of Great Britain - 62 acres of land, part of "Hitt or Miss." Acknowledged before Robert Lloyd and Joseph Sudler. Alienation fine,
two shillings, six pence sterling.

062. 2 August 1744 - 16 August 1744   William Vickers of Talbot County,
Planter, to my daughter Sarah Herrington of Queen Anne's County -
in consideration of love and affection I bear unto her - "Warner's
Discovery," now in the possession of her husband Anthony Herrington;
he to have use of it for life and afterwards to Sarah and her heirs.
Acknowledged before Robert Lloyd and James Brown. Alienation fine,
eight shillings sterling, paid by Anthony Herrington.

062. 31 July 1744 - 16 August 1744   William Osburn of Kent Island, to John
Smyth - leases for a term of twenty years, land called "Martain's
Neck" on the Island - left to me by my father William Osburn in his
will; patented to him 20 May 1725 and now in Smyth's possession by
virtue of an indenture to him for five years made between him and the
said William Osburn, in the custody of Thomas Barns of Kent Island,
which indenture is now void. Yearly rent is 100 pounds of tobacco.
Wits: John Walters, Edward Reveling. Acknowledged before William and
Edward Tilghman.

063. 28 August 1744   James Baley to George Jackson, Blacksmith - consideration 1,000 pounds of tobacco - 50 acres in the forrest called "Try-
angle." Acknowledged before Robert Norrest Wright and Associates.
Alienation fine two shillings sterling.

064. 6 August 1744 - 28 August 1744   John Certain and ____ his wife to
James Massy - consideration 4,200 pounds of tobacco - 85 acres, part
of "Friendship" - adjoining part sold by Coll. Tilghman to Francis
Spry - lying on Unicorn Branch. Acknowledged before William Tilghman
and Humphery Wells, Jr. Alienation fine, three shillings, five pence
sterling paid to Richard Tilghman.

065. 10 April 1743 - 1 September 1744   Thomas Chaires and William Elbert,
appointed by Thomas Wilkinson to view and value 66 acres, part of
"Waltham" and "Wilkinson's Addition," the property of John Denny, a
minor - Thomas Hynson Wright his guardian - find two old dwelling houses; two old tobacco houses; one old corn house; all very much out of
repair; one small old orchard and two-thirds of the cleared ground
under mean fencing. The annual value 640 pounds of tobacco clear of
quitrents and necessary repairs; the guardian allowed to get timber
for necessary repairing and to clear any land within the fence and
not elsewhere except for tobacco hogsheads.

066. 1 September 1744   Elizabeth Hawkins, Gentlewoman, to William Wrench,
Planter - consideration 21,101 pounds of tobacco - 326 acre, part of
"Hawkins Farm Resurveyed" on Coursica Creek. Acknowledged before
William Tilghman and Humphery Wells, Jr. Alienation fine, thirteen
shillings, one-half penny sterling.

067.   1 September 1744   Elizabeth Hawkins, Gentlewoman, to Abraham Oldson, Planter - consideration 8,156 pounds of tobacco - 126 acres,
part of "Hawkins Farm Resurveyed." Acknowledged before William
Tilghman and Humphery Wells, Jr. Alienation fine, five shillings,
one-half penny sterling paid to Richard Tilghman.

068.   1 September 1744   Elizabeth Hawkins to Peter Countice, Planter -
consideration 7,767 pounds of tobacco - 120 acres, part of "Hawkins
Farm Resurveyed" on Coursica Creek - adjoining Ambrose Wright.

069.   30 August 1744 - 8 September 1744   John Croney and Mary his wife,
Planters, to Edward Jumpe, Planter - consideration 3,500 pounds of
tobacco - 50 acres called "Godfrey's Folly," formerly laid out for
Godfrey Viney of Queen Anne's County, now in the possession
of Edward Jumpe - lying on the east side of Tuckahoe Creek and adjoining "New Buckby," formerly laid out for John Wooters of Talbot
County. John and Mary (she being first privately examined) acknowledged before Robert Lloyd and William Hopper. Alienation fine, two
shillings sterling.

071.   4 April 1744 - 20 September 1744   John Tully of Summerset County,
heir at law of Stephen Tully, formerly of Queen Anne's County (or
that part of Talbot County so-called) as is proved by the deposition
of Stephen Tully, son of the aforesaid Stephen Tully, deceased, and
James Tully, uncle to the said heir John Tully, aforesaid, to Henry
Coventon, Planter - consideration 6,000 pounds of tobacco - 100 a-
cres, the unsold part of "Providence," on the west side of Tuckahoe
Creek - adjoining John Miller's land. John Tully and James Tully
acknowledged before Robert N. Wright and William Hopper. Alienation
fine, six shillings, three pence sterling.

072.   13 June 1744 - 20 September 1744   Anne Butler, Widow, to John Rogers
of Kent County (Md.), Planter - Marriage Contract - about to be wed
on or before the 30th day instant, Anne agrees with John in case of
her decease before him to give him part of "Chesterfield" during his
lifetime; in return if widowed, she gets one-half of his land. Acknowledged before Robert N. WRight and William Hopper.

073.   8 August 1744 - 23 September 1744   Henry Raveland of St. Mary's Coun-
ty, Province of Maryland, Planter, and Elizabeth his wife, to Samuel
Massey of Chester Town in Kent County (Md.), Hatter - consideration
£40 current money - one-half of 100 acres of land devised by George
Ayres, deceased, to the aforesaid Elizabeth his daughter. Wits:
Thomas Aisquith, Philip Clarke, Justices of the Peace, St. Mary's
County; certified by Richard Ward Key, Clerk, 15 August 1744. Alien-
ation fine, two shillings sterling paid to Richard Tilghman.

074.   29 August 1744 - 8 October 1744   Ernault Hawkins, Planter, to Elizabeth Hawkins, Widow - consideration 20,000 pounds of tobacco - a
parcel of land on the south side of Chester River heretofore in Kent
County but now in Queen Anne's - part of "Tully's Delight," lying on
the east side of Island Creek, devised to Ernault Hawkins by his
grandfather, John Hawkins, 23 April 1717.

62.

075. 18 August 1744 - 1 November 1744 James Powell, Planter, and Mary
Anne his wife, to Richard Cook, son and heir of Hercules Cook, deceased - consideration 2,500 pounds of tobacco - 20 acres of land,
part of "Partnership" - on the south side of Double Creek Branch.
James and Mary Anne (she being first privately examined) acknowledged
their deed before James Brown and Humphery Wells, Jr. Alienation
fine, 10 pence sterling, paid to Richard Tilghman.

076. 4 August 1744 - 28 November 1744 Edward Willoughby, Planter, and
Mary his wife, to John Jackoman of Talbot County, Wheelwright - consideration ₤2 current money and 5,000 pounds of tobacco - 100 acres,
the dwelling plantation of Edward Willoughby - part of "Sawyer's
Addition" adjoining "Branfield," taken up by Peter Sawyer and sold
to Johannes Dehenyosia of Queen Anne's formerly Talbot County. Edward and Mary (she being first privately examined) acknowledged before Robert Lloyd and Henry Casson. Alienation fine, four shillings
sterling.

077. 4 December 1744 Sarah Burke, Widow, to Thomas Boone and Sarah his
daughter - a gift of love and affection - to Thomas, a servant man
named James Rose; a large Bible; two featherbeds and their furniture;
two iron pots; one looking glass; three pewter dishes; two spinning
wheels; one large chest; two cows and calves. To Sarah, a young mare
called "Fortune:" one ewe and lamb; one pied heifer; one young sow.
Wits: Henry Casson, Nathaniel Knotts.

078. 22 November 1744 - 20 December 1744 Thomas Hynson Wright and Mary
his wife, to John Lloyd - consideration 8,000 pounds of tobacco -
132 acres, part of "Tom's Fancy Enlarged," in Tully's Neck. Thomas
and Mary (she being first privately examined) acknowledged before
Robert Norrest Wright and William Hopper.

079. 10 December 1744 - 20 December 1744 Ernault Hawkins, Planter, and
Jane his wife, to Christopher Cox, Gentleman - consideration 1,200
pounds of tobacco - 38 acres, part of "Prophecy," lying on the west
side of the Southeast Branch of Island Creek - adjoining a part formerly in possession of Joseph Earle, Sr. and "Readbourn." Ernault
and Jane (she being first privately examined) acknowledged before
Thomas Hynson Wright and William Hopper. Alienation fine, eight
pence half penny sterling paid to Richard Tilghman.

081. 13 November 1744 - 26 February 1744 Milinton Sparks, Planter, to
Absalom Sparks, Planter - consideration 5,000 pounds of tobacco -
part of "Sparkes's Enclosure," part of "Sparkes's Choice," on Island
Creek, bequeathed to Milinton Sparks by his father John Sparks. Acknowledged by Milinton Sparks and Mable his wife before Robert Norrest
Wright and William Hopper. Alienation fine, three shillings, eleven
pence sterling.

081. 13 November 1744 - 26 February 1744 Calep Sparks, Planter, to Absalom Sparks, Planter - consideration 3,000 pounds of tobacco - part
of "Sparkes's Enclosure" and part of "Sparkes's Choice" on Island

63.

081. Creek - bequeathed to him by his father John Sparks. Acknowledged
     before Robert Norrest Wright and William Hopper. Alienation fine,
     three shillings, eleven pence sterling, paid to Richard Tilghman.

082. 15 January 1744 - 26 February 1744 Charles Conner, Planter, to
     Elizabeth Clouds, Widow - 15-year lease of 15 acres, part of "Wood-
     yard Thicket," on Kent Island, at ten shillings per annum. Elizabeth
     to have liberty of cutting timber for a dwelling house. Wits: James
     Harvey, William Osburn, Mary Griffith. Acknowledged before James
     Brown and Joseph Sudler.

083. 16 January 1744 - 26 February 1744 Nathaniel Reed of St. Paul's
     Parish, Carpenter, to his daughter Mary Reed - a gift of love - 300
     acres, part of "Tom's Fancy Enlarged" - adjoining "Smith's Forrest."
     Acknowledged before R. N. Wright and William Hopper.

084. 13 November 1744 - 26 February 1744 John Parsons, Planter, and
     Catharine his wife, to Thomas Tate, Planter - consideration 3,000
     pounds of tobacco - 30 acres, part of "Mary's Chance," on Beckleses
     Branch of Chester River - near "Wyatt's Lott." John and Catharine
     (she being first privately examined) acknowledged before James Brown
     and Humphery Wells, Jr.

085. 1 December 1744 - 26 February 1744 Christopher Wilkinson and Eliza-
     beth his wife, to Michael Earle, Mariner - consideration ₤30 current
     money and ₤10 in the hands of Richard Tilghman for the use of the
     said Elizabeth - 100 acres, part of "Emory's Fortune Addition" -
     adjoining the land of John Emory; John Blades' cornfield; Hopper's
     and the land of William Emory. Christopher and Elizabeth (she being
     first privately examined) acknowledged before William Tilghman and
     James Brown.

086. 30 November 1744 - 28 February 1744 Matthew Reed of Kent County,
     and Henrietta his wife, to Thomas Hynson Wright, Gentleman - consid-
     eration 16,000 pounds of tobacco and ₤5 current - 100 acres, part of
     "Gray's Inn," lately bought of Thomas Hynson Wright. Matthew and
     Henrietta (she being first privately examined) acknowledged before
     Charles Downes and Henry Casson.

087. 11 February 1744 - 12 March 1744 Daniel Willcocks, Planter, to James
     Willcocks, Planter - consideration 10,000 pounds of tobacco - 95
     acres, part of "Mounthope," on Island Creek - adjoining "Rawlins'
     Chance" and George Elliott's Landing. Daniel and Hannah his wife,
     acknowledged before Robert Norrest WRight and William Hopper. Alien-
     ation fine one shilling, eleven pence sterling, paid to R. Tilghman.

088. 26 March 1745 Benjamin Boone, Planter, to Richard Chance, Planter -
     consideration 5,000 pounds of tobacco - 30 acres near the Choptank
     River called "Garding of Roses" and "Boon's Hope" - adjoining "Little-
     worth," on Dickinson's Branch. Alienation fine, one shilling, three
     pence sterling.

089. 6 February 1744 - 28 March 1745 Michael Miller of Kent County, Planter, to Peregrine Frisby of Cecill County, Gentleman - consideration
₺280 current money and 10,000 pounds of tobacco - two tracts of land
on Kent Island; "Crawford," lying near the mouth of Craney Creek -
adjoining "Cooper's Freehold," 248 acres; the other, "Cooper's Freehold," originally surveyed for Robert Cooper on the west side of Kent
Island, bounded on the west by Chesapeake Bay; on the south by Andrew
Basha(?) and James Houghton; on the east by the path leading to Beaver Neck - 80 acres. Acknowledged before B. Hands and John Williamson, Justices of the Peace for Kent County; certified by James Smith,
Clerk. Alienation fine, six shillings, nine pence, three farthings
sterling, paid to Richard Tilghman.

091. 25 March 1745 - 29 March 1745 Thomas Wilkinson to William Hopper -
consideration ₺70 current - quitclaim on 100 acres, part of 200 acres
called "Providence," purchased from Esther Banbury - on the Chester
Mill Branch. Wits: Thomas Hynson Wright, Nathan Samuel Turbutt
Wright. Acknowledged before Robert Norrest Wright and James Brown.
Alienation fine, two shillings sterling.

092. 28 February 1744 - 10 April 1745 Absalom Sparks, Planter, to John
Earle, Planter - consideration 7,000 pounds of tobacco - part of
"Sparkses Enclosure," per the will of his father John Sparks; and a
part of the same bought of his brother Milinton Sparks, 13 November
last; and part bought of Calep Sparks - lying on Island Creek. Acknowledged before Robert Norrest Wright and William Hopper. Alienation fine, eleven shillings, nine pence sterling.

093. 3 April 1745 - 10 April 1745 Nathaniel Read and Sarah his wife, son
and devisee of Matthew Read, deceased, who was the eldest son and devisee of Matthew Read, late of TAlbot County, to Thomas Hynson Wright -
in consideration of 300 acres now conveyed, part of "Tom's Fancy Enlarged" and ₺50 sterling money - 100 acres whereon Nathaniel Read
now dwells, the remaining part of "New Reading." Acknowledged before
William Tilghman and William Hopper. Alienation fine two shillings,
sterling.

094. 4 April 1745 - 10 April 1745 Thomas Hynson Wright, Gentleman, to
John Downes, Jr. - consideration 3,000 pounds of tobacco - 40 acres
in the Long Neck, called "Wright's Reserve." Wits: William Tilghman, William Hopper. Alienation fine one shilling, seven pence.
sterling.

095. 29 March 1745 - 11 April 1745 James Chaires and Margarett his wife,
to William Pratt, Planter - consideration 6,000 pounds of tobacco -
54 acres, part of "Chairs Addition," on the head of Corsica Creek
Branch - adjoining "Walnut Ridge." James and Margarett (she being
first privately examined) acknowledged before Charles Downes and
William Hopper.

096. 13 February 1744 - 13 April 1745 John Neavil, Planter, and Anne his
wife, to John Powel, Planter - consideration 6,000 pounds of tobacco -

096. 94 acres, "Powell's Fancy," lying in ye Forrest of Choptank on ye
Little Beaver Dam Branch. John Nevil and Anne his wife (she being
first privately examined) acknowledged before James Brown and Humphery Wells, Jr. Alienation fine, three shillings, nine pence sterling, paid to Richard Tilghman.

097. 13 February 1744 - 13 April 1745 John Nevil and Anne his wife, to
John Powel - consideration 3,000 pounds of tobacco - 50 acres called
"Long's Desire," lying in the freshes of Choptank River on the north
side of Beaver Dam Branch. Acknowledged before James Brown and Humphery Wells, Jr. Alienation fine, two shillings sterling.

099. 11 February 1744 - 25 April 1725 James Wilcocks to Daniel Wilcocks,
Planter - consideration 10,000 pounds of tobacco - 100 acres, part
of "Mounthope" - on Island Creek. Acknowledged before Robert Norrest Wright and William Hopper. Alienation fine, four shillings sterling.

099. 2 May 1745 Nathaniel Tucker, Planter, and Neriah his wife, to Christopher Cox, Planter - consideration 2,340 pounds of tobacco - 39
acres, part of "Adventure" - adjoining the land of the Rev. Mr.
James Cox. Nathaniel and Neriah (she being first privately examined) acknowledged before William Tilghman and Joseph Sudler. Alienation fine, one shilling, seven pence sterling paid to R. Tilghman.

101. 13 December 1744 - 24 May 1745 Thomas Hinesly, Planter, and Rachel
his wife, to John Clothier, Planter - consideration 3,500 pounds of
tobacco - part of "Hinesly's Plains" in Tully's Neck, sold by Thomas
Hinesly to my father, Nathaniel Hinesly, except what was sold by my
father to Edward Roe and William Scandrett - reputed to be 64 acres.
Thomas and Rachel (she being first privately examined) acknowledged
before Robert Norrest Wright and William Hopper. Alienation fine,
two shillings, seven pence sterling.

102. 1 April 1745 - 20 June 1745 Henry Price, Planter, and Elizabeth his
wife, to Robert Blunt, Planter - consideration 15,000 pounds of tobacco - 373 acres on White Tree Branch between Choptank River and
Tuckahoe Creek in Tuckahoe Neck - called "Copartnership." Elizabeth
released her dower rights. Henry and Elizabeth (she being first privately examined) acknowledged before Robert Lloyd and William Tilghman. Alienation fine, fourteen shillings, eleven pence sterling.

104. 15 June 1745 - 25 June 1745 John Casson, Merchant, and Mary his
wife, to Henry Feddeman, Planter - consideration ₤65 current - 100
acres, part of "Hackett's GArden" - on the east side of Tuckahoe
Creek. John and Mary (she being first privately examined) acknowledged before Edward Tilghman and Henry Casson. Alienation fine,
four shillings sterling.

105. 25 June 1745 Elisha Mannery of Talbot County, Planter, and Henney
his wife, to Isaac Thorpe, Planter - consideration 2,000 pounds of
tobacco - part of "Cole Raine," bequeathed by James Jordan to his

105. daughter, Henny Jordan - part of "Cole Raine" on the west side of
Tuckahoe Creek. Elisha and Kenney (she being first privately examin-
ed) acknowledged their deed before Robert Lloyd and William Hopper.
Alienation fine, eight pence sterling, paid to Richard Tilghman.

106. 11 June 1745 - 9 July 1745 Thomas Wyatt of Kent County, Delaware,
and Mary his wife, to Jacob Bell, Carpenter - consideration 4,000
pounds of tobacco - 50 acres, part of "Wyatt's Range" lying on the
east side of Hogg Pen Swamp in Long Neck. Wits: James Brown and Edward Tilghman - before whom Thomas and Mary acknowledged (she being
first privately examined out of his hearing).

108. 9 July 1745 Thomas Davis, Planter, to Richard Tilghman, Gentleman -
consideration ₤138.8.0 current money - part of "Content," whereon I
now live - on the south side of the main road leading by my plantation and east of the fresh run that lyes back of my dwelling house;
and all of "Beaver Dams," purchased of Edward Wright; and all of "Hollow Flat," purchased of Thomas Bostock - a mortgage. Acknowledged
before Robert Norrest Wright and William Hopper.

109. 15 July 1745 Nathaniel Hunt, Planter, to Anna Maria Tilghman - consideration 1,765 pounds of tobacco and 13 shillings, 3 pence current
money -- one young horse called "Snip;" one called "Diamond;" three
sows, two calves and two yearlings; and all hoggs with the increase
of the cattle and hoggs. A mortgage due 10 October next. Wits:
William Tilghman, Thomas Ringgold. Acknowledged before W. Tilghman.

110. 14 February 1744 - 15 July 1745 Etheldred Davy, late of the City of
Exon, Kingdom of Great Britain, now of Talbot County, to William Thom-
as of Talbot, Gentleman - consideration ₤90 sterling money of Great
Britain - all the lands in Tuckahoe Creek purchased from John Baynard,
Henry Feddeman and Elizabeth Feddeman, with one house thereon and all
the tobacco belonging to the said Davy now in the house. Wits: Ris-
don Bozman, James Edge, John Goldsborough, who witnessed Davy's re-
ceipt to Thomas for the money paid by James Tilghman. John Leeds,
Clerk, certified Bozman and Edge as Justices of the Peace for Talbot
County. Alienation fine, four shillings, two pence sterling.

111. 19 March 1744 - 15 July 1745 John Dempster to John Tittle of Kings
Town in Queen Anne's County, Shoemaker - consideration ₤5 current -
lot Number Twenty-one in Kings Town. Wits: James Brown, Humphery
Wells, Jr. - before whom Dempster acknowledged.

111. 15 July 1745 Robert Walters and Elizabeth his wife, of Kent Island,
to their son Jacob Walters - a gift of love and affection - 90 acres
of land where Alexander Walters now lives - near the Wading Place
and adjoining "Allen's Decept" (sic!). Wits: Alexander Walters,
Joshua Walters. 20 March 1745 Acknowledged before Robert Lloyd and
James Brown.

112. 8 March 1744 - 15 July 1745 William Scandrett, Sr. and Johana his
wife, Planters, to their son William Scandrett, Jr., Mariner - a

112. a gift of love - part of "Lexton," on Coursica Creek. (No acreage given). Acknowledged before William Tilghman and William Hopper.

113. 28 February 1744 - 17 July 1745 William Scandrett, Jr., Mariner, to Thomas Caradine, Planter - Power of Attorney to settle his accounts, 23 February 1744. Acknowledged before William Hopper.

113. 17 July 1745 Henry Downes, Planter, to Thomas Perkins and Samuel Cockayne of Talbot County, Planters - consideration ₤37.12.6 - 158 acres, part of "Carter's Forrest" - adjoining "Wilton Addition" now in the possession of Richard Bennett; John Emerson's part of "Carter's Forrest;" and "Noble's Range." Wits: James Tilghman, William Tilghman. Acknowledged before Charles Downes. Alienation fine, six shillings, four pence sterling, paid by James Tilghman.

114. 20 May 1745 - 18 July 1745 Marian Powell, Widow, to John Nevill - consideration 7,000 pounds of tobacco - 78 3/4 acres, part of "Tilghman's Discovery," near the head of Double Creek. Acknowledged before James Brown and Humphery Wells, Jr.

115. 18 July 1745 Samuel Cockayne, Planter, and Thomas Perkins to Henry Downes, Planter - consideration ₤37.12.6 current silver or gold of America - 158 acres, part of "Carter's Forrest." Alienation fine, six shillings, four pence, paid to Richard Tilghman.

116. 18 July 1745 Richard Tilghman to John Dempster - release of the mortgage given 8 May 1742 in the amount of ₤230 - for part of "Poplar Hill" (excepting the part laid out for Kings Town) - 498 acres. Wits: John Webb, James Tilghman. Acknowledged before Edward Tilghman, William Hopper.

117. 19 July 1745 - 20 July 1745 Christopher Wilkinson to Joseph Tryall and John Gwin - two featherbeds and furniture; three pewter dishes; three basons; four plates; two iron potts and hooks; two potracks; four trunks; two large chests; one gray mare and yearling; one brown mare and horse colt; four sows and piggs; three barrows and all my part of my plantation whereon I now live as also the tract called "Fair Dealing" in Kent County near the head of Chester River, 170 acres on Cyprus Branch. They my security for ₤12.9.10 sterling and cost of suit due to Mrs. Bridget Donaldson at Annapolis - provided Wilkinson shall pay her. Acknowledged before William Hopper.

117. 20 July 1745 - 25 July 1745 Thomas Hynson Wright, High Sheriff of Queen Anne's County, to Charles Browne, Merchant - the goods of Thomas Baily, Jr., late of Queen Anne's County, Planter, taken by Writ of Attachment 10 April past, to the value of 8,000 pounds of tobacco - a parcel of land called "part of Bradburn's Delight otherwise Bailey's Delight;" 100 acres on a cove of Coursica Creek. Wits: John Tilden, Jr., John Emory. Acknowledged before Robert Lloyd and William Hopper. Alienation fine, four shillings sterling paid to R. Tilghman.

118. 12 April 1745 - 20 August 1745 Richard Bennett, Gentleman, to Rich-
ard Mollineau of Charles County, Gentleman - two tracts surveyed for
John Lundy and patented to his (Bennett's) mother, Henrietta Maria
Lloyd: "Batchelor's Plains," 216 acres on the east side of Unicorne
Branch; the other, "John's Forrest," 200 acres on the west side of
the Unicorne Branch; also three tracts John Lundy devised to Henri-
etta Maria Lloyd: "Lundy Resurveyed," 200 acres on the south side of
Red Lyon Branch; "Woodhouse," 300 acres on the east side of Unicorne
Branch and "Waterford," 200 acres on the west side of Pearle's Creek,
Chester River. Wits: Robert Lloyd and Edward Tilghman - before whom
Bennett acknowledged. Alienation fine, forty-four shillings, eight
pence paid to Richard Tilghman.

119. 28 August 1745 James Cox, Gentleman, to John Nabb, Planter - consideration ₤7 current - 7 acres, part of "Adventure." Acknowledged before James Brown and Joseph Sudler. Alienation fine, three pence,
halfpenny sterling.

119. 29 August 1745 John Baynard, Merchant; Thomas Baynard, Planter, and
John Baynard, son of William, Planter, to each other - 500 acres,
"Pitts' Vineyard," the land of John Baynard of Talbot County, deceas-
ed, their grandfather - on the east side of Tuckahoe Creek in Talbot
County but now in Queen Anne's. Mention John Baynard's will of
13 November 1704 in which he devised the land to his three sons, Thom-
as, Robert and William, to be divided between them by the Quakers of
Thirdhaven Monthly Meeting - and which was never done. Wits: Robert
Norrest Wright, Joseph Sudler. Acknowledged before R. N. Wright and
Associate Justices. Richard Tilghman, Clerk.

122. 10 August 1745 - 29 August 1745 John Mollis, Planter, to Edward
Bruer - consideration 1,800 pounds of tobacco - one cow and calf; a
parcel of hoggs; the crop of Indian corn and tobacco now growing and
the old corn I now have; fowls; and all of my household goods. Wit:
Edward Downes.

122. 29 August 1745 - 30 August 1745 John Wooters, Planter, to Thomas
Swann, Planter - consideration 300 pounds of tobacco - 2½ acres of
land, part of "Jump's Choice," lying on the main road formerly called
St. Jones' Path - in the fork between Tuckahoe Creek and Choptank Riv-
er. Wits: Charles Downes, John Davis. Acknowledged before Charles
Downes and Henry Casson. Alienation fine, one pence farthing.

123. 2 August 1745 - 30 August 1745 Marmaduke Goodhand and James Sudler
evaluate the land of Morris Sliney who has 'chuse' Dr. John Smyth
his guardian. Found on the dwelling plantation one 36 by 18 feet
dwelling house with brick gable ends and shimbleys, planked above and
below, one room plastered; one 15 foot square kitchen with posts in the ground; one good
tobacco house 40 by 20 feet with posts in the ground; one 12 foot
corn house, log'd; 1292 pannells of old fencing and 89 apple trees,
belonging to the home plantation - likewise a small tenement on the
same neck of land where there is a 20 foot dwelling, 16 feet wide,

123. very old and much out of repair; one very old tobacco house, 30 by
20 feet and 366 pannells of fencing, very old and 9 apple trees.
The land is very poor and swampy and we value two-thirds of the plantation as Morris Sliney has a mother in law living, which a third belongs to her, to be worth 800 pounds of tobacco yearly; Dr. Smyth to
have timber for necessary repairs. Goodhand and Sudler certified by
Joseph Sudler, 2 August 1745.

124. 31 August 1745 Jane Ross, Widow, to Charles Goldsborough - consideration 2,500 pounds of tobacco - four cows and calves; two 4-year
old horses, now on her plantation. Acknowledged before James Brown.

124. 8 August 1745 - 31 August 1745 Richard Wells and Francis Rochester
evaluate the estate of Bexley John Lambdin, son and heir of George
Lambdin, deceased; an orphan under the care of John Swift, his guardian. The land is "Lambdin's Adventure," all cleared and under fence
except four or five acres, chiefly swampy scrubby land and a few scrubby trees. Found one dwelling house, 25 feet long, sheded on one side,
much out of repair in the roof; one old dwelling, round loggs, small
and not worth repairing; one old dwelling in the pasture, 20 by 15
feet, bastard framed, much out of repair; one tobacco house, 30 by 20
feet, sheded on one side, in midling good order; one old tobacco house,
bad in the cover and shed broke down; one corn house, 12 feet long,
square loggs and doftailed, new and good; one old cornhouse and a meat
house, round loggs, new and a good roof, 12 feet long; and a reasonable good well with a wooden frame. There is also a likely young orchard about 114 apple trees and many vacancys and a likely nursery to
supply, each in a separate fence; also an old field plot in fence,
about 6,000 corn hills; an old field pasture adjoining, of 8,000 or
10,000 corn hills, with 4 apple trees, 10 cherry trees and a few old
peach trees in it and a corn field adjoining them of about 20,000
hills and another corn field on the other side of the orchard of about
15,000 hills; a stubblefield adjoining of about 16,000 corn hills.
There is those separate enclosures besides tobacco ground, all midling
good fence some part, with old rails far wore. The yearly rent of
1,000 pounds of tobacco to be reduced to 250 pounds since there is
much needed repairing.

125. 26 August 1745 - 2 September 1745 John Dempster, Planter, to Samuel
Massey of Kent County, Hatter - consideration ₤250 current money -
234 acres, part of "Poplar Hill" on Fishing Creek, Chester River (except such part of Kingstown as is already sold; also lott Number Ten
in the town). John Dempster and Joan his wife acknowledged before
James Brown and Humphery Wells, Jr. Alienation fine, five shillings,
eight pence sterling.

126. 27 August 1745 - 12 September 1745 John Dempster, Planter, to John
Nevill, Planter - consideration ₤236 current - part of "Poplar Hill,"
234 acres (except part of Kings Town already sold to John Nevill).
John and Joan Dempster acknowledged before James Brown and Humphery
Wells, Jr. Alienation fine, four shillings, eight pence sterling.

128. 14 October 1745 - 18 October 1745 Thomas Wilkinson to Joseph Tryall -
consideration 3,000 pounds of tobacco and ₤7 current money - negro
man named "Parismus," now in the possession of Mr. Thomas Hynson
Wright and under Vincent Vanderford as Overseer. Wits: Thomas Dodd
and John Wilkinson. Acknowledged before William Hopper.

128. 24 October 1745 - 28 October 1745 James Hollyday to his son James
Hollyday, Jr. - a gift of love - a parcel of land conveyed to me by
John Hawkins, Jr. and Sarah his wife, 4 February 1734 - part of "Mack-
linborough." Wits: Henry Hollyday, John Courdly.

128. 5 November 1745 - 8 November 1745 John Hamer, Planter, to Samuel
Massey of Kent County, Hatter - 300 acres called "Chestnut Neck" on
Dividing Creek, Chester River - adjoining "Poplar Hill" and Fishing
Creek. Wits: Lambert Wilmer, George Garnett. Acknowledged before
James Brown and Humphery Wells, Jr. - A lease.

129. 6 November 1745 - 8 November 1745 John Hamer, Planter, to Samuel
Massey of Kent County, Hatter - consideration ₤295 current money -
"Chestnut Neck." Alienation fine, six shillings sterling, paid to
Richard Tilghman.

130. 6 November 1745 - 27 November 1745 Samuel Massey of Kent County, Hatter, to Henry Cully, Gentleman - consideration ₤27 current money - 27
acres, part of "Poplar Hill" (formerly the property of John Dempster);
beginning at the lowermost corner of Kings Town at the corner of Henry
Cully's lot - adjoining John Nevill's part. Samuel and Sarah Massey,
his wife, acknowledged before James Brown and Humphery Wells, Jr.
(Sarah being first privately examined). Alienation fine, seven pence
sterling.

132. 29 November 1745 John Tillotson, Gentleman, to William Bishop, Planter - release of 136 acres called "Mill Range" in Talbot County but
since the division now in Queen Anne's - west side of the southern
branch of Coursica Creek - reference to Writ of Entry obtained August
1745, Tillotson vs Bishop. Acknowledged before Robert Lloyd and William Hopper.

132. 29 November 1745 John Legg, Sr. to his daughter Mary Legg - a gift
of love and affection - a moiety of the land where I dwell called
"Oulson's Relief" - adjoining "Barrent Ridge" - after my death. Reversion to son John Legg, Jr. in case of the death of Mary without
issue. Acknowledged before Robert Norrest Wright and Humphery Wells,
Jr. Alienation fine, two shillings sterling paid to Richard Tilghman.

134. 30 November 1745 William Bishop, Planter, to Margaret Ward of Talbot
County, Widow - consideration ₤22 sterling - 136 acres, a tract of
plantable land called "Mill Range," on the west side of the southern
branch of Corsica Creek. Acknowledged before James Tilghman and William Hopper.

134. 22 November 1745 - 30 January 1745 Mary Hudson of Kent County on
Delaware, daughter of John Stark late of Talbot County, Widow, and
Michael Toole, Planter, to John Bayley, Sr., Planter - consideration
1,200 pounds of tobacco - 100 acres, part of "Bayly's Delight" but
originally called "Bradburn's Delight" - on Coursegall Creek. Acknowledged before Charles Downes and William Hopper. Alienation fine,
four shillings sterling paid to Richard Tilghman.

135. 13 February 1745 - 27 August 1745 Michael Hacket of Kent County,
Province of Maryland, Planter, to Valentine Thomas Honey, Planter -
consideration 5,000 pounds of tobacco - 100 acres, part of "Mitchell's
Adventure," on the southeast side of Island Creek - adjoining "Mt.
Hope" - part of the same tract sold by Michael Hacket, grandfather to
Michael Hacket, present grantor, to William Sparks - adjoining "Tull-
y's Delight." Acknowledged before James Brown and Humphery Wells,
Jr. Alienation fine, two shillings sterling.

137. 8 November 1745 - 3 March 1745 Peter Massy, Sr., of Kent County,
Province of Maryland, Planter, and Jane his wife; Nicholas Massy, Sr.,
Planter, of Kent County and Katherine his wife; James Massy of Queen
Anne's County, Planter, and Rachel his wife to Peter Massy, Jr. of
Kent County, Maryland, Carpenter - consideration 6,200 pounds of to-
bacco - 140 acres, "Johnson's Adventure" with "Massy's Hazard," on
Unicorn Branch. Acknowledged before James Brown and Humphery Wells,
Jr. (the wives being previously examined). Alienation fine, five
shillings, seven pence sterling, paid to Richard Tilghman.

138. 25 October 1745 - 3 March 1745 James Ridley of Salem County, Province
of West New Jersey, Sawyer, to William Robinson, Planter - consideration 10,000 pounds of tobacco - 200 acres, "Ridley's Chance," lying
on Elliott's Branch. Acknowledged before Robert Norrest Wright and
William Hopper. Alienation fine, eight shillings sterling.

139. 27 February 1745 - 3 March 1745 Elizabeth Hawkins, Widow, to William
Dockery (also Dockura) - consideration 1,200 pounds of tobacco paid
by Thomas Hynson Wright - 8 acres, part of "Hawkins' Farm," on the
north side of Chester Mill Branch. Wits: James Harvey, Benjamin Kir-
by. Acknowledged before Robert Lloyd and William Tilghman. Alienation fine, four pence sterling.

140. 14 February 1745 - 3 March 1745 Nathan Wright, Planter, son and heir
at law of Edward Wright, deceased, to Robert Sumpter, Planter - consideration 2,000 pounds of tobacco paid to Edward Wright in his lifetime - 50 acres, "Watery Plains" - between Choptank River and Long
Marsh. Wits: Thomas H. Wright, Matthew Dockery. Acknowledged before
Thomas Hynson Wright and William Hopper. Alienation fine, two shillings sterling.

141. 24 January 1745 - 25 March 1745 Thomas Harris and Nathan Wright,
appointed to value 50 acres of land called "Smeath," the right of
John King Beck, a minor, William Emory, his guardian. Find eight
acres cleared; a tobacco house, 30 by 20 feet, very old and decayed.

141. The guardian to pay a yearly rent of five pounds of tobacco without privilege of clearing any more ground. Acknowledged before Edward Tilghman.

141. 18 January 1745 - 26 March 1746 Isaac Dixon of Talbot County, Planter, to his brother, John Dixon of the same place - part of the land called "Jerusalem," willed to him by their father, Isaac Dixon of Talbot County, deceased. Acknowledged before Perry Benson and W. Thomas, Justices of the Peace for Talbot County; certified by John Leeds, Clerk. Alienation fine, eight shillings sterling.

142. 3 April 1746 William Till of the City of Philadelphia and Mary his wife, to Thomas Hynson Wright - consideration five shillings - one-year lease for part of "Winton," lying on the west side of Coursica Creek, 500 acres - "Winton's Addition," 50 acres on the north side of Winchester's Branch - and 25 acres, part of "Winton's Addition," in Coursica Creek near the head of Macklin's Branch - and 500 acres, part of "Park," at the head of Double Creek. Wit: William Bingham, William Moore, Jr.

143. 3 April 1746 - 7 April 1746 William Till of the City of Philadelphia and Mary his wife, to Thomas Hynson Wright - by virtue of a statute for transferring uses into possession and the sum of two shillings - conveyes title to the above lands. Wit: William Bingham, William Moore, Jr. Alienation fine, one pound, one shilling, six pence sterling.

143. 7 February 1745 - 10 April 1746 William Rickord and Mary his mother and Sarah Rickord his wife, to William Green, Planter - consideration 9,000 pounds of tobacco and £8 current money - 100 acres, "Bradford" - lying on John Elliott's Branch, Island Creek. Acknowledged before William Hopper and James Brown (Mary and Sarah being first privately examined). Alienation fine, four shillings sterling, paid to Richard Tilghman.

145. 8 March 1745 - 10 April 1746 Richard Bennett, Esquire, to William Emory, Jr., son of John Emory, Blacksmith - for a valuable consideration and the further sum of five shillings - 287 acres, part of "Wingfield," lying in the fork of the fresh runs of Tuckahoe Creek - originally surveyed for Col. Vincent Lowe for 1,000 acres. Acknowledged before Robert Lloyd and Edward Tilghman. Alienation fine, eleven shillings, six pence sterling.

145. 21 March 1745 - 20 April 1746 Christopher Granger to his daughter Sarah Granger, of my wife Anne by me, born before our marriage - a gift of love - negro boy called "Will," four years old. Acknowledged before Thomas Hynson Wright and Joseph Sudler.

146. 15 November 1745 - 24 April 1746 Thomas Hynson Wright, Gentleman, High Sheriff of Queen Anne's County, to Richard Wells, Planter, and Mary his wife, only child and representative of George Hollyday, late of Queen Anne's County - 50 acres, "Williams' Adventure" - reference

146. to a Writ of Entry against Edward Williams and Mary his wife, als
Mary Hollyday, to the value of b400 sterling and 5,000 pounds of tobacco. Acknowledged before Charles Downes and William Hopper.

147. 21 November 1745 - 27 May 1746 William Shurmer, Yoeman, of Kent
County on Delaware, son of Benjamin Shurmer of ye county, deceased,
to Waitman Sipple, Sr. of the said county, Yoeman - consideration
b100 current money - three tracts of land deemed to be in the Province of Maryland in Queen Anne's County, laid out for Benjamin Shurmer. One, called "Tappahanna" begins at a small island at the head
of a great marsh at the head of the main branch of Choptank River,
called Tappahanna Marsh, containing 1,370 acres. Another tract of
250 acres is called "Spicy Grove;" and the other is "Land of Benjamin's" - 275 acres adjoining "Winterfield" - formerly laid out for
William Comegys at the head of Tappahanna Marsh. Acknowledged before
James Brown and Humphery Wells, Jr.

148. 12 February 1745 - 27 May 1746 John Hartshorne, Carpenter, and Elizabeth his wife, to Thomas Nickison (Nicholson), Planter - consideration 7,000 pounds of tobacco - 100 acres, part of "Woodhouse" on
Unicorne Branch and 25 acres adjoining called "Woodhouse Addition."
John and Elizabeth acknowledged (she being first privately examined)
before James Brown and Humphery Wells, Jr. Alienation fine, five
shillings sterling, paid to Richard Tilghman.

149. 29 May 1746 John Baynard, Jr., son of William, and Mary his wife, to
William Bancks, Merchant - consideration b80 current - 165 2/3 acres,
part of "Pitts' Vineyard," east side of Tuckahoe Creek - adjoining
"Hacker's Garden." John and Mary (she being first privately exam-
ined) acknowledged before Thomas Hynson Wright and William Tilghman.
Alienation fine, six shillings, eight pence sterling.

151. 19 April 1746 - 20 May 1746 William Diggs of Prince George's County,
Gentleman, son of Charles Digges, Gentleman, deceased, to Thomas
Price, Planter - consideration 9,000 pounds of tobacco - 123 acres,
part of "Branford" on Tuckahoe Creek. Wits: B. Young, James Tilghman. Acknowledged before Benjamin Young. Alienation fine, four
shillings, eleven pence sterling.

151. 7 April 1746 - 24 June 1746 Robert Whorton and Joseph Newnam, sworn
by Humphery Wells, Jr. to value the land of William Bussell, son and
heir of John Bussell, deceased, who died possessed of the land called "Philadelphia," containing 50 acres - find one dwelling house,
20 x 16 feet, hewed logs, much out of repair; one milk house, 12 x 10
feet, framed, in middling repair; one old schoolhouse, round loggs,
very much out of repair; one little new house, 12 x 10 feet, round
loggs, rough, indifferent work; one tobacco house, 30 x 20 feet, bastard framed, in good order; one tobacco house. the whole frame in indifferent repair; one tobacco house, 20 feet square, old fashioned or
posts in the ground, very much decayed in the roof; one corn house,
12 x 6½ feet, shingled roof in very good order; one old decayed hen
house; 660 pannells of fence, some seven and some eight rails high,

151. chiefly old rails and much out of repair; 75 apple trees; 35 peach
trees; 32 cherry trees, 6 middling good and 26 small scrubbs; a water
well, 15 feet deep, a logg frame, much out of order - and as Margaret
Bussell the widow, is in living, the quitrents and repairs considered, we value the yearly rent at 300 pounds of tobacco and limit Charles Lowder the guardian, to clear no more than two acres per year;
one acre in ye branch and one on high land.

152. 22 June 1741 - 30 June 1746 John Dempster to Henry Cully of Chester
Towne in Kent County, Merchant - leases 12 acres, part of "Poplar
Hill," adjoining Kings Town and Lot Number One or the Prize House
Lott - runs along the river to Fishing Creek. For the life of Henry
Cully and Christian his wife and the life of David Dempster, son of
John.

6 November 1745 This lease was transferred to Samuel Massey. Wits:
James Brown, Humphery Wells, Jr., George Garnett.

153. 24 July 1746 Richard Blunt, Planter, and Robert Blunt, Carpenter, to
Samuel Blunt, Planter - an additional portion of "Great Neck" on Kent
Island, above the part given to Samuel in a division made 25 Novemb-
er 1736 of 110 acres. (No acreage). Acknowledged before Robert
Lloyd and Charles Downes.

154. 21 March 1745 - 15 August 1746 Christopher Granger and Ann his wife,
of Kent Island, Planter, to John Willson, Planter - consideration
£66 paper currency - 20 acres, a couple of small islands called Emerson's Islands - in the mouth of Eastern Creek. Christopher and Ann
(she being first privately examined) acknowledged their deed before
Thomas Hynson Wright and Joseph Sudler. Alienation fine, ten pence
sterling, paid to Richard Tilghman.

155. 19 July 1746 - 15 August 1746 Richard Hammond of Talbot County,
Planter, to Thomas Cooper, Innholder - consideration 3,000 pounds of
tobacco - a lot in Queens Town - adjoining the lot where Thomas Cooper
lately lived belonging to Richard Tilghman, Esquire - left to Hammond
by his father, 27 January 1717. Richard and Sophia his wife, acknowledged before Thomas Hynson Wright and William Tilghman.

156. 2 June 1746 - 15 August 1746 Richard Blunt of Kent Island, Planter,
to Robert Blunt, Planter - consideration £30 paper currency - 110
acres, part of "Great Neck." Wits: Robert Lloyd and Joseph Sudler.
Alienation fine, two shillings, two and one-half pence sterling.

158. 17 June 1746 - 15 August 1746 Elizabeth Hawkins, Widow, to Richard
Bennett, Esquire - leases part of "Hawkins Farm Resurveyed, 20 acres;
"Bowlingly," 250 acres; "Macklin," 100 acres; "Beaver Damms," 160
acres; "Green Spring," 650 acres; part of "St. Paul's," 50 acres;
part of "Carman's Neck," 100 acres; "Forrest Lodge," 152 acres; part
of "Knowles' Range," 256 acres; "Partnership," 400 acres; "Discovery,"
220 acres; part of "Tully's Delight," 200 acres - for a term of one
year, for the purpose of securing to Bennett for purchase.

75.

158. 18 June 1746 - 15 August 1746 Elizabeth Hawkins, Widow, and Edward
Neale of Prince George's County, enter into a Marriage Contract.
Acknowledged before Thomas Hynson Wright and Charles Downes.

160. 16 July 1746 - 20 August 1746 Ernault Hawkins, Planter, to his
daughters in law, Mary Smith Andrew and Catherine Frances Andrew - a
gift of love. To Mary S., a negro girl named "Marina" at age eighteen, a negro boy named "Polydore" at my decease. To Catherine F.,
a negro girl named "Violet" at age eighteen, and a negro girl named
"Dorcus" at my decease - to each or the survivor. Wits: Thomas Wilkinson, William Bishop. Acknowledged before Robert Norrest Wright
and William Hopper.

160. 3 June 1746 - 21 August 1746 William Digges, Prince George's County,
Gentleman, to Thomas Price, Planter - consideration 600 pounds of tobacco - 6 acres, part of "Blanford." Wits: Benjamin Young, Benjamin
Young, Jr. William and Anne his wife, (she being first privately examined) acknowledged before Benjamin Young. Alienation fine three
pence sterling, paid to Richard Tilghman.

161. 18 August 1746 - 21 August 1746 William Bishop, Gentleman, to Thomas
Hynson Wright and William Hopper, Gentlemen - part of "Smith's Mistake" (reference to a mortgage made 20 December 1742.) Acknowledged
before Robert N. Wright and Charles Downes.

162. 25 July 1746 - 21 August 1746 William Mason, Planter, to John Davis,
Jr., Planter - consideration 3,000 pounds of tobacco - 32 acres called "Peale Place" on the Beaver Dam Branch, Choptank River - and 68
acres called "Addyhouse" on the Beaver Dam Branch. William and Anne,
his wife, (she being first privately examined) acknowledged before
Robert Norrest Wright and William Tilghman.

163. 18 July 1746 - 27 August 1746 Richard Bennett, Merchant, to John
Young, son of William, Planter - consideration 2,000 pounds of tobac-
co - 50 acres, part of "Stratton." Wits: J. Loockerman, Jr., Thomas
Clarke. Acknowledged before Robert Lloyd and Edward Tilghman.
Alienation fine, two shillings sterling.

164. 18 July 1746 - 27 August 1746 Richard Bennett, Merchant, to John
Young, Planter - consideration 2,180 pounds of tobacco - 54½ acres,
part of "Stratton." Acknowledged before R. Lloyd and E. Tilghman.
Alienation fine, two shillings sterling.

165. 18 July 1746 - 27 August 1746 Richard Bennett, Merchant, to William
Young, Planter - consideration 2,080 pounds of tobacco - 52 acres,
part of "Stratton." Alienation fine, two shillings, one pence sterling.

166. 3 June 1746 - 27 August 1746 William Digges of Prince George's County, Gentleman, to Robert German (Jarman), Jr., Planter - consideration
18,990 pounds of tobacco - 211 acres, part of "Branford," on the west
side of Tuckahoe Creek. William and Anne, his wife, acknowledged before Benjamin Young. Alienation fine, eight shillings five pence half

166. penny sterling, paid to Richard Tilghman.

167. 27 August 1746 William Shurmer, Yoeman, of Kent County on Delaware,
      son of Benjamin Shurmer, to Weightman Sipple, Sr., Yoeman - consid-
      eration ₤100 current money - three tracts of land deemed to be in
      Queen Anne's County, Province of Maryland - "Tappahanna," 1,370
      acres; "Spicy Grove," 250 acres and "Land of Benjamin," 275 acres.
      Acknowledged before James Brown and Humphery Wells, Jr.

169. 11 June 1746 - 27 August 1746 Thomas Benton, Planter, and Sarah his
      wife, and Mary Taylor to John Legg, Jr., Planter - "Pentroby," 14
      acres on Kent Island, in exchange for "Limbrick," "Legg's Beginning"
      and five shillings. Acknowledged before Joseph Sudler and Edward
      Tilghman. Alienation fine, three shillings, half penny sterling,
      paid to Richard Tilghman.

169. 28 August 1746 John Luxon of Bideford, County Devon, England, Mer-
      chant and Thomas Kenney of the same place, Merchant, executors of the
      will of John Buck late of Bideford, Merchant, deceased, to Captain
      John Marten of Bideford, Mariner and Master of the good ship, "Mary-
      land Merchant" - Power of Attorney to settle Buck's accounts. Wits:
      William Priest and William Bishop. Sworn to by Priest before James
      Brown, 28 August, 1746.

170. 30 August 1746 Richard Porter, Jr., Chirurgeon, to Edward Tilghman,
      Gentleman - consideration ₤100 paper - negro woman, "Phillis;" negro
      boy, "Chester;" negro girl, "Phillis;" negro girl, "Daphne" and a
      negro boy, "Joseph." (a mortgage). Wit: Patrick McGuire. Acknow-
      ledged before Robert Norrest Wright.

171. 29 August 1746 - 30 August 1746 William Wilkinson and John Scotten
      of Queen Anne's County, Planters, to Matthew Tilghman of Talbot Coun-
      ty, Gentleman - consideration 2,000 pounds of tobacco - 50 acres,
      part of "Glocester," on the north side of Andover Branch, Chester
      River. Wits: William Tilghman, Thomas Elliott. Acknowledged before
      Joseph Sudler and Humphery Wells, Jr.

172. 18 July 1746 - 30 September 1746 Richard Bennett, Merchant, to John
      Scott, Planter - consideration 21,300 pounds of tobacco - 532½ acres,
      part of "Stratton" on Tuckahoe Creek. Wits: J. Loockerman, Jr., Thom-
      as Clarke. Acknowledged before Robert Lloyd and Edward Tilghman.

173. 18 July 1746 - 30 September 1746 Richard Bennett, Merchant, to Solo-
      mon Scott, Planter - consideration 12,440 pounds of tobacco - 311
      acres, part of "Stratton."

173. 3 June 1746 - 9 October 1746 William Digges of Prince George's Coun-
      ty, Gentleman, to John Meads, Planter - consideration 14,100 pounds
      of tobacco - 141 acres, part of "Blanford," adjoining Stephen Yoe's
      part. Wits: B. Young, B. Young, Jr. William and Anne his wife (she
      being first privately examined) acknowledged before Benjamin Young.
      Alienation fine, five shillings, eight pence sterling.

77.

174. 3 June 1746 - 9 October 1746 William Digges of Prince George's County to Amos Jarman, Planter - consideration 3,700 pounds of tobacco -
25 acres, part of "Blanford," adjoining John Meads and 12 acres, adjoining "St. Martins" (originally taken up by Coll. William Digges).
Alienation fine, one shilling, six pence sterling.

175. 3 June 1746 - 16 October 1746 William Digges of Prince George's County to William Mead - consideration 10,000 pounds of tobacco - 100
acres, part of "Blanford" - adjoining "St. Martins." Alienation fine,
four shillings sterling.

176. 3 June 1746 - 16 October 1746 William Digges of Prince George's County to Stephen Yoe, Planter - consideration 10,000 pounds of tobacco -
100 acres, part of "Blanford" - adjoining Robert Jarman, Jr. Alienation fine, four shillings sterling.

177. 26 September 1746 - 21 October 1746 William Watson, Province of
Pensilvany and Roberta his wife, to Richard Blunt, Planter - consideration ₤30 Maryland money - 50 acres in the Forrest of Choptank -
part of "Long Marsh Ridge" - near the Long Marsh. Acknowledged before
James Brown and Humphery Wells, Jr. Alienation fine, two shillings
sterling.

178. 22 September 1746 - 23 October 1746 Katherine Hammond, Widow, to her
daughter Mary, wife of Tobais Stansbury of Baltimore County, Merchant -
gift of "Robinson's Farm, " 200 acres; also negro woman "Heby," with
her four children: "Nan," "James," "Sarah" and "Panola." Wit: W.
Bond. He and Charles Crooke witnessed Katherine's receipt to Tobias
Stansbury on behalf of his wife. Confirmed by John Brerewood, Clerk
of Baltimore County.

179. 11 June 1746 - 24 October 1746 John Legg, Jr., Planter, and Rachel
his wife, and Penelope Wright to John Legg, Planter - 14 acres, part
of "Limbrick" and "Legg's Beginning," on Kent Island - in exchange for
land called "Pentroby" and one shilling paper money. Adjoining John
Leggs' "Woodland Neck." John and Rachel his wife (she being first
privately examined) acknowledged before Joseph Sudler and Edward
Tilghman. Alienation fine, seven pence sterling.

180. 29 August 1746 - 24 October 1746 Thomas Hynson Wright to Edward
Brown - consideration ₤40 current - 150 acres, part of "Tom's Fancy
Enlarged," adjoining Charles Lizenby's part; John Lloyd's and Thomas
Meloyd's and Nathaniel Read's. Acknowledged before Robert Norrest
Wright and James Brown. Alienation fine, six shillings sterling.

181. 23 October 1746 - 24 October 1746 Thomas Hammond, Jr., son and heir
of Jane Hammond, deceased, to Richard Tilghman, Gentleman - consideration ₤120 current money - 200 acres called "Cheshire," the real estate of Thomas Hammond, Sr. and part of the "Plains," 105 acres.
Wits: John Brice, Thomas Williamson. Thomas and Sarah his wife acknowledged before John Brice, a Justice of the Provincial Court.

182. 9 September 1746 - 11 November 1746 Richard Porter of Talbot County, Chirurgeon, and Alice his wife, to Matthew Tilghman, Gentleman -
consideration ₤100 - 500 acres called "Timber Neck" on Andover Branch.
A mortgage, due 9 September 1749. Acknowledged before John Goldsborough and Thomas Porter, Justices of the Peace - confirmed by John
Leeds, Clerk of Talbot County.

183. 27 October 1746 - 19 November 1746 William Hopper, Gentleman, to
Thomas Emory, Planter - consideration ₤200 - 150 acres, part of "Partnership," lying near the head of Coursey's Creek (reference to a
parcel of escheat land adjoining and John Emory). Mary Anne Hopper
relinquished her right of dower and acknowledged with her husband
before Thomas Hynson Wright and Charles Downes (having first been
privately examined out of his hearing). Alienation fine, six shillings sterling, paid to Richard Tilghman.

185. 27 October 1746 - 13 November 1746 Arthur Emory, Planter, to his son
Thomas Emory, Planter - a gift of the land called "Emory Paxton" on
the west side of Thomas' Branch between "Rosseth" and "Walker's
Square," containing 100 acres. Acknowledged before Thomas Hynson
Wright and Charles Downes. Alienation fine, four shillings sterling.

185. 1 October 1746 - 27 November 1746 John Scott to Robert Wharton -
consideration 1,020 pounds of tobacco - 17 acres, part of "Sayer's
Range Addition," on the Red Lyon Branch. Acknowledged before Thomas
Hynson Wright and James Brown.

186. 10 June 1746 - 28 November 1746 Richard Bennett to Edward Roe, Plan-
ter - consideration 5,740 pounds of tobacco - 164 acres, part of
"Oakenthorpe," on the fresh runs of Tuckahoe Creek - adjoining John
Miller's and "Wright's Chance" (now possessed by Nathaniel Wright);
and "Tully's Addition," (now possessed by Edward Roe). Wits: Thomas
Clarke and John Loockerman, Jr. Acknowledged before John Darnall,
Justice of the Provincial Court. Alienation fine, six shillings,
seven pence sterling.

187. 25 November 1746 - 29 November 1726 Thomas Hynson Wright, Gentleman, to Benjamin Chaires, Planter - consideration 10,000 pounds of
tobacco - 100 acres, part of "Warplesdon Addition" and "Solomon's
Friendship." Acknowledged before James Brown and Joseph Sudler.
Alienation fine, four shillings sterling.

188. 25 November 1746 - 29 November 1746 Thomas Hynson Wright to Thomas
Meloyd, Planter - consideration 3,000 pounds of tobacco - 100 acres,
part of "Tom's Fancy Enlarged." Acknowledged before Joseph Sudler
and James Brown. Alienation fine, four shillings sterling.

189. 30 August 1746 - 29 November 1746 Thomas Hynson Wright to Thomas
Newton - consideration 3,600 pounds of tobacco - 100 acres, part of
"Tom's Fancy Enlarged," adjoining the land of George Smith. Wits:
James Reid, John Wright. Acknowledged before Robert Norrest WRight
and Charles Downes. Alienation fine, four shillings sterling.

190. 30 October 1746 - 4 December 1746 Alice Wright to her daughter,
Mary Ann Wrench - a negro girl named "Judy;" to daughter, Mary Anne
Wright - a negro boy, "Pompey;" to son, Edward Wright, a negro girl,
"Hannah;" to son Nathaniel Wright, a negro girl, "Jane;" to daughter,
Rachel Wright, a negro boy, "Coffee;" to daughter, Dorothy Fairclough
Wright, a negro girl, "Daphne." Acknowledged before Thomas Hynson
Wright and Charles Downes.

190. 5 December 1746 - 1 January 1746 Richard Bennett, Merchant, to Littleton Ward, Cooper - consideration 22,880 pounds of tobacco - 286
acres, part of "Colne Rectified," lately patented - on the east side
of Tuckahoe Creek near the Cattail Pond - adjoining Henry Pollock.
Acknowledged before James Brown and N. Wright, Jr. Alienation fine,
eleven shillings, five pence half penny sterling.

192. 6 January 1746 George Lewis, Planter, to Richard Tilghman - consideration ₺75 current - 75 acres, part of "Boaquely" - on Coursica Creek,
adjoining "Bennett's Regulation." George Lewis to settle any differ-
ence regarding the line between him and Thomas Chaires. Acknowledged before Thomas Hynson Wright and N. Wright, Jr.

193. 29 December 1746 - 8 Janaury 1746 William Dulany, Planter, to Thomas
Harris, Planter - consideration ₺52.5.0 current money and 8,959
pounds of tobacco - 200 acres called "Standford," on the west side of
Thomas's Branch - adjoining "Mt. Mill" (laid out for Robert Morris),
"Middle Plantation" and the land of William Young. Also part of
"Mt. Mill," containing 60 acres. Acknowledged before Thomas Hynson
Wright and N. Wright, Jr.

194. 4 November 1746 - 10 January 1746 William Roberts and Elizabeth his
wife, to John Emory, Planter - consideration 7,500 pounds of tobacco -
150 acres, "Roberts' Range" - on the northeast branch of Choptank
River near the Beach Ridge. Also part of "Roberts' Range Addition,"
37 acres, granted 27 September 1743. Elizabeth Roberts relinquished
her dower and acknowledged with her husband before James Brown and
Humphery Wells, Jr. (she being first privately examined). Alienation
fine, seven shillings, six pence sterling.

196. 2 September 1746 - 5 February 1746 Jacob Hindman of Talbot County,
Gentleman, to John Jackson, Phisician - release of land called "Lexon"
on Corsica Creek (an attachment) and one messuage thereon - devised
by Roger Weddel als Woodal to his oldest son, Thomas Woodal. Acknowledged in September 1745 before Thomas Bozman and W. Thomas, of
Talbot County.

197. 5 February 1745 Richard Tilghman to Baldwin Kemp - Receipt for an
alienation fine of three shillings, eight pence sterling, paid for
the deed recorded in R.T. No. B, folios 303, 304, and 305.

197. 25 November 1746 - 5 February 1746 John McConnikin and Mary his
wife, Planter, to William Willson, Planter - consideration ₺320 paper
currency - 327 acres, part of "McConnikin's Fortune" - at the head

197. of Wallis' Marsh. John and Mary (she being first privately examined) acknowledged before Thomas Hynson Wright and Humphery Wells, Jr. Alienation fine, thirteen shillings, one pence sterling, paid to Richard Tilghman.

199. 11 FEbruary 1746 - 19 February 1746 Winifred Ford, Widow of William Ford, to Francis Rochester, Jr. - two iron gray mares; one red and white cow; a white cow yearling; one featherbed, rug and bedstead - in payment of the sum of £8.12.9. Wits: John Forakers, Thomas Mounseer. Acknowledged before Humphery Wells, Jr.

200. 4 February 1746 - 19 February 1746 Henrietta Maria Robins of Talbot County, Widow of George Robins, Gentleman, to Thomas Stewart, Planter - 105 acres, a moiety of "Sylvester's Forrest" in Tuckahoe Neck, also 90 acres adjoining, one-half of "Larey's Discovery," which George Robins purchased of Charles Loud, 25 March 1741. Originally sold to Thomas Stewart and Thomas Martingale for 11,000 pounds of tobacco - Martingale having declined, Mrs. Robins assigns to Thomas Stewart. Acknowledged in Talbot County before Thomas Bullen and Jeremiah Nicols; confirmed by John Leeds, Clerk. Alienation fine, seven shillings, two pence sterling.

201. 21 February 1746 - 28 February 1746 Jacob Bell, Carpenter, and Margaret his wife, to John Furbush - consideration 4,000 pounds of tobacco - 50 acres called "Wyatt's Range," on the side of Hog Pen Swamp in Long Neck. Jacob and Margaret (she being first privately examined) acknowledged before N^n. Wright, Jr. and James Brown.

202. 8 December 1746 - 26 February 1746 William Ellis of Kent County, Carpenter, to William Barkhurst, Planter - consideration 4,000 pounds of tobacco - 80 acres, part of "Golden Ridge," on the south side of Chester River. James Brown and Humphery Wells, Jr. Alienation fine, three shillings, two pence sterling.

203. 20 October 1746 - 12 March 1746 William Osburn of Kent Island, to John Smith, Surgeon (also written Smyth) - consideration 35,000 pounds of tobacco - 113½ acres, one-half of "Martin's Neck," on Martin's Creek, Kent Island. Acknowledged before Thomas Hynson Wright and Robert Norrest Wright. Alienation fine, four shillings, six pence half penny sterling.

204. 27 January 1746/7 - 12 March 1746 William Coursey, Gentleman, and Rachel his wife, to John Holden, Planter - lease of "Sleeford" and "Sheppard Hook," whereon John Haly now lives, for a term of fifteen years; at 800 pounds of tobacco per annum. Holden to build a tobacco house, 40 x 20 feet, double ground tyr'd with a girder through the middle and well braced, this to be a framed house. One more tobacco house 40 x 22 feet with posts in the ground and bastard framed to be double ground tyr'd; the covering boards for both houses to be well drawn and sapt and the weather boards well drawn; and one framed 20 foot dwelling house. Holden to forfeit 10,000 pounds of tobacco if not completed. Wits: Edward Clayton, Samuel Walters.

205. 27 March 1746 - 28 March 1746 William Elbert, Gentleman, to George
Lewis, Planter - Release of a Writ of Entry made September 1746 on
50 acres of land called "Lewis's Chance," on Courseca Creek, on
Boaques Branch adjoining the "Reward," formerly laid out for Robert
Macklin; "Boaquely," formerly laid out for John Boaque." Acknow-
ledged before Humphery Wells, Jr. and William Clayton.

206. 27 March 1747- 28 March 1747 George Lewis and Sarah his wife, to
William Elbert - consideration ₤30 current money and 1,500 pounds of
tobacco - "Lewis's Chance," 50 acres. Alienation fine, two shillings
sterling paid to Richard Tilghman.

207. 16 March 1746 - 28 March 1727 Isaac Ford, Planter, and Mary his wife
to Edward Jones - consideration 17,000 pounds of tobacco - 30 acres,
"Ford's Park," in the forrest between the branches of Chester and
Choptank Rivers - beginning on the west side of the Horsehead and by
the path that leads from Chester to St. Jones's. Also 100 acres called "Hopewell," lying near Ford's dwelling plantation and 20 acres,
"Ford's Folly." Acknowledged by Isaac and Mary (she being first privately examined) before James Brown and Humphery Wells, Jr. Alienation fine, six shillings sterling.

208. 24 March 1746 - 28 March 1747 Thomas Hynson Wright, Gentleman, to
John Pratt, Planter - consideration 10,000 pounds of tobacco - 100
acres, "Wright's Park," adjoining "Content," now ih possession of
Thomas Golt and Edward Wright. Acknowledged before James Brown and
Humphery Wells, Jr. Alienation fine, four shillings sterling.

209. 25 March 1747 - 28 March 1747 William Elbert, Gentleman, to Susannah Douglas of Kent County, Widow and executrix of George Douglas,
Gentleman - consideration five shillings - 500 acres of land on Red
Lyon Branch called "Macklin's Phancy," in consideration of a bond
given to George Douglas. Wits: John Webb, James Tilghman, Acknowledged before Thomas Hynson Wright and Associates.

210. 28 March 1747 Jonathon Nicols, Justice, appointed John Burke and
Thomas Fisher to view and value the land and plantation of Daniel
Cox, a minor (Jarvis Langfitt, his guardian) - entered on 22 December 1746 and found one clapboard dwelling house, 20 x 15 feet in
good repair; one framed tobacco house, 30 x 20 feet in good repair;
a young orchard of about 70 apple trees; 400 pannells of fencing.
The guardian is to clear four acres of woods and pay the orphan the
sum of 450 pounds of tobacco per annum.

211. 26 February 1746 - 28 March 1747 Benjamin Falkner and Mary his wife,
of Dorchester County, Planters, to John Burke, Planter - consideration 1,200 pounds of tobacco - 50 acres, a moiety of "Falkner's Lott"
on Tuckahoe Creek - adjoining "Nottenham," laid out for John Wig-
gins. Benjamin and Mary (she being first privately examined) acknowledged before Nm. Wright, Jr. and Jonathon Nicols.

212. 26 March 1747 - 28 March 1747 Alexander Toalson, Planter, and Susanah his wife, to Benjamin Toalson, Planter - consideration 7,800
pounds of tobacco - 100 acres, part of "Coppedge's Range" on Kent Island. Wits: Joseph Sudler, James Brown. Alexander and Susanah acknowledged before Sudler and Brown, Susanah being first privately
examined out of hearing of her husband. Alienation fine, four shillings sterling, paid to Richard Tilghman.

213. 26 March 1747 - 28 March 1747 George Lewis, Planter, to Richard
Tilghman, Gentleman - consideration ₤20 current money of the Province
and 6,967 pounds of tobacco - all his part of "Boaquely" on Coursica
Creek, about 61 acres - a mortgage due 10 November 1749. Wits: N.
Wright, Jr., Richard Tilghman Earle. William Elbert witnessed Lewis'
receipt to Tilghman. George and Sarah Lewis his wife, (she being
first privately examined) acknowledged before N^n. Wright, Jr. and
Nathan Wright.

214. 28 March 1747 John Stevens and William White, appointed by Joseph
Sudler to value the land of Thomas Price, son of Andrew Price, deceased, find: one dwelling house 24 x 18 feet with brick gable end
to the chimney, old and much out of repair; one very old citching,
very much out of repair hasan outside brick chimney; one good 40 x
20 tobacco house, double tier'd; one 30 x 20 feet tobacco house single tier'd, old; one small logged corn house, very old and bad; 1,132
pannells of old fencing and six apple trees; the land much broken
and swampy and is very poore. The guardian to cleare any land he
thinks proper and permitted to get timber for raills and boards for
repairs and cooper's timber for the plantation. We value two-thirds
of the plantation to be 600 pounds of tobacco yearly.

215. 29 December 1746 - 28 March 1747 John Stevens and William White,
appointed by Joseph Sudler to value the land of Samuel Griffith who
'choused' James Sudler for his guardian, find: one old dwelling
house, 20 x 16 feet, plank floor much out of repair; a citching adjoining said dwelling, 25 x 16 feet in pretty good repair with a
small entry; one outroom, 20 x 16 feet, plank floor below, old; one
40 foot tobacco house, pretty old; one small loged house, 12 x 8
feet in good repair; one stable, 20 x 12 feet in good repair; one
loged corn house, 16 x 8 feet in good repair; one 8 foot square
milk house, framed work in pretty good repair; 66 apple trees and
1,044 pannells of fencing, part very good. On another plantation one
loged house, 20 x 16 in pretty good repair; one loged corn house, 10
feet long in very good repair; 652 pannells of old fencing. The
guardian to clear anything within the fencing of the plantation last
mentioned; to get timber for rales and boards to repair the plantation and houses and tobacco hogshead timber. The dwelling plantation valued to 1,000 pounds of tobacco yearly and the other ar 600
pounds of tobacco.

215. 28 March 1747 Christopher Phillips and Robert Phillips, Planters,
to Richard Tilghman, Gentleman - in consideration of five shillings
and a lease for certain lands during the natural life of Christopher

215. and Hannah his wife, to be made by the said Richard Tilghman - all of "Smith's Lott," at the head of Reed's Creek, containing 200 acres according to patent. Wits: James Brown, Richard Tilghman Earle. Acknowledged before James Brown and Joseph Sudler.

216. 26 March 1747 - 28 March 1747 Hynson Wright, Planter, and Sarah his wife with Mrs. Neriah Jones, John Pickering and Anne his wife, to Edward Jones, Planter - consideration 10,700 pounds of tobacco and ₤6 paper currency - a tract of land called ye "Beginning," lying in the main fork of Tuckahoe Creek and near the head of the northernmost main branch, containing 85 acres. Wits: William Clayton, James Wrench. Acknowledged before Thomas Hynson Wright and William Clayton, Sarah Wright and Anne Pickering having first been privately examined. Alienation fine, three shillings, five pence sterling, paid to Richard Tilghman.

217. 26 March 1747 - 28 March 1747 Thomas Lane of Talbot County, Gentleman, and Mary his wife, to William Jarman - consideration 7,500 pounds of tobacco - 125 acres, all of "Hogharbour," lying near the head of the northeastern main branch of Tuckahoe Creek on the east side of Long Marsh - beginning at the head of a little swamp near the Bee Tree Marsh (except about nine acres on the north side which an older survey called "Hemsley's Discovery" takes from it). Warranted against the dower of Mary, wife of Charles Downes, Gentleman. Wits: William Clayton, Robert Lloyd. Acknowledged by Thomas and Mary (she being first privately examined) before Thomas Hynson Wright and William Clayton. Alienation fine, five shillings.

218. 5 December 1746 - 2 April 1747 Richard Bennett, Merchant, to Henry Pollock of Talbot County, Shipwright - consideration ₤113.12.0 - current money of the Province - 284 acres, part of "Colne Rectified," lately patented to Richard Bennett - lying on the east side of the main branch of Tuckahoe Creek on the south side of Cattaile Pond - mention a division line between Pollock and Littleton Ward who has also purchased the other part of the said land. Acknowledged before James Brown and N^n. Wright, Jr. Alienation fine, eleven shillings, four pence half penny.

220. 31 March 1747 - 18 April 1747 Joseph Tryall, Carpenter, to Thomas Caradine, his bondsman - four cows and three yearlings. Wits: Thomas Wilkinson, Thomas Wilkinson, Jr. Acknowledged before William Clayton.

220. 14 April 1747 - 21 April 1747 John Knowles and Anne his wife, to Thomas Hynson Wright - consideration 2,500 pounds of tobacco - part of "Kendall," late the right of Thomas Owens, deceased. John and Anne (she being first privately examined) acknowledged before Nathan Wright and N^n. Wright, Jr.

220. 4 November 1746 - 21 April 1747 Humphry Wells, Gentleman, to Thomas Stanton, Planter - consideration 6,000 pounds of tobacco - 100 acres of land called "Security," lying between the head of Long Marsh and and Beaver Dam Marsh - adjoining "Forrest of Sherwood," now in the

220. possession of Thomas Stanton. Humphery and Elizabeth his wife (she being first privately examined) acknowledged before James Brown and Humphery Wells, Jr.

221. 9 March 1746 - 30 May 1747 James Troth of Talbot County, Planter, to James Tilghman of Talbot County, Gentleman - consideration 4,500 pounds of tobacco - 300 acres, all of "Cole's Banks" on Choptank River, and 100 acres, "Cole's Banks Addition." Acknowledged before James Edge and John Coward, Justices of Talbot County; certified by John Leeds, Clerk of Talbot County. Alienation fine, sixteen shillings sterling paid to Richard Tilghman.

222. 18 June 1747 John Forbush, Planter, to Richard Tilghman - consideration 4,000 pounds of tobacco and twenty shillings current money of Maryland - 50 acres, all of "Wyatt's Range," on the east side of Hogpen Swamp in Long Neck. John and Esther his wife (she being first privately examined) acknowledged before Thomas Hynson Wright and Nathan Wright.

223. 2 June 1747 - 21 June 1747 John Rogers to Thomas Butler - lease of the plantation whereon Rogers now dwells - 200 acres on the north side of Coursica Creek, part of "Chesterfield" - beginning February last and during the natural life of John Rogers and Ann his wife - the rent, 1,500 pounds of tobacco yearly; Thomas agreeing to pay arrears of quitrents. Acknowledged before Thomas Hynson Wright and William Clayton.
3 June 1747 John Rogers assigned two years rent to Thomas Hynson Wright for the consideration of 2,300 pounds of tobacco. Wits: John Smith and William Clayton.

224. 15 June 1747 - 23 June 1747 Thomas Wyatt of Kent County, Delaware, to John Swift - consideration 10,000 pounds of tobacco - 100 acres, part of "Low's Desire," lying on the north side of Red Lyon Branch, adjoining the land sold to Thomas Hadaway by George Hadaway out of the said tract. Acknowledged before James Brown and Humphery Wells, Jr. Alienation fine, four shillings sterling, paid to R. Tilghman.

225. 23 June 1747 John Newnam, Planter, to Joseph Elliott, Planter - consideration 4,500 pounds of tobacco - 50 acres, all of "Newnam's Hermitage," lying on Unicorn Ridge - patented to Daniel Newnam, 1 July 1723 - also 10 acres called "Williams' Lott," lying near "Newnam's Hermitage." John and Rachel his wife (she being first privately examined) acknowledged before James Brown and Humphery Wells, Jr. Alienation fine, two shillings, five pence sterling.

226. 26 June 1747 - 9 July 1747 Thomas Baley and Hannah his wife, to Banarde Tillotson, Planter - consideration 8,000 pounds of tobacco - 100 acres, all of "Exchange." Thomas and Hannah (she being first privately examined) acknowledged before N^n. Wright, Jr. and William Clayton. Alienation fine, four shillings sterling.

228. 13 July 1747 - 23 July 1747 Samuel Taylor to Thomas Hynson Wright -

228. reference made to a deed written 8 October 1736 for 100 acres, part of "Lowe's Arcadia," which was not delivered by Wright to be enrolled by the County Clerk within six months - for which reason Wright now requireth a further confirmation. Acknowledged before James Brown and N^n. Wright, Jr.

228. 24 April 1747 - 23 July 1747 Francis Rochester and James Massey, appointed and sworn by Humphery Wells, Jr. to view and value the land and plantation of Bexley Newnam, a minor, son of Joseph Newnam, deceased, who 'dyed' possessed of "Shearing" with the "Addition" and part of "John's Meadow" - found a 30 foot brick dwelling house, a shed on one side, the window shutters much broken but otherwise in good repair; a 20 foot 'citchin' with brick chimney, old, in midling repair; one 15 foot milk house, old and in midling repair; a 10 foot square logg'd meat house, midling good; 2 40 foot tobacco houses with a shed to each, very old and much out of repair; two 15 foot corn houses, old and indifferent; a good framed well about 20 feet deep and a good brick oven; 140 apple trees, some scrubby quince and peach trees and 18 cherry trees; 1,330 pannells of fencing, some 8 and some 9 rails high, chiefly old, standing in midling good order and a cross fence between Daniel Newnam and this plantation to be kept up, containing 196 pannells, some 8, some 9 rails high, old but standing in good order. On another plantation on "Newnam's Adventure," found one dwelling house, one part very old and all in poor order; 8 apple trees; 8 peach trees and 2 cherry trees; 229 pannells of fencing, about 8 rails high with some poles and 33 pannells of fencing about the same height, all poles; and as Sarah Newnam, widow of Joseph Newnam is in being and the quitrents considered, valued the annual rent to be 800 pounds of tobacco per annum and as the greater part of the principal seat of land is under fence we limmit William Newnam, the guradian, that he clear but on the southeast side of the plantation and that in the swamps and neckes within the fence first and don't exceed one acre in any one year, that being for tobacco beds and fire wood. William Newnam not to clear more than one-half acre a year of "Newnam's Adventure." Valuation made at the request of William Newnam, guardian to Bexley Newnam.

229. 14 August 1747 - 24 August 1747 Jane Parnes, Widow, to Humphery Wells, Jr. - consideration 800 pounds of tobacco - 100 acres of land, her right to "Jenny's Beginning" which is chiefly taken away by an older survey, being a tract called "Bath," belonging to Humphery Wells, Sr. - lying between the Red Lyon and Unicorn Branches and adjoining "Constantinople." Acknowledged before James Brown and N^n. Wright, Jr. Alienation fine, four shillings sterling.

231. 30 May 1747 - 25 August 1747 Thomas Hynson Wright to James Finley, Wheelwright - consideration 5,000 pounds of tobacco - 50 acres, part of "Solomon's Friendship" and "Warplesdon Addition" - adjoining His Lordship's Mannor. Acknowledged before Nathan Wright and William Clayton. Alienation fine, two shillings sterling.

232. 24 August 1747 - 25 August 1747 Michael Hussey, Planter, to Henry and John Casson - consideration 1,400 pounds of tobacco - two cows, 2 'calfs' and one year old. Wits: Jonathon Nicols, Mary Nicols. Acknowledged before Jonathon Nicols.

233. 12 July 1747 - 27 August 1747 Rebecka Costin, Widow, to her son, James Costin - gift of love - one 'molatto' girl about fourteen years, after her death. James agreed not to put Rebecka to her thirds of the dwelling plantation but to provide for her house and room and to procure what tobacco and 'grane' she can make on the said plantation during her lifetime. If the said molatto girl should have increase before she comes into the hands or possession of James Costin or his heirs, the increase is to be to the whole disposing of Rebecka to whom she shall think fit. Wits: Peter Garron, Frances Downes, Henry Downes.

233. 13 April 1747 - 28 August 1747 Thomas Chaires and Thomas Wilkinson, appointed and sworn by Thomas Hynson Wright to view and value the land of John Taylor, a minor with Thomas Dodd, his guardian, 90 acres called "Batchelor's Hope" and 51 acres called "Neglect," found one framed dwelling house 24 x 18 feet with a brick chimney, an earthen floor below and no floor above; one old dwelling house 28 x 18 feet, very much out of repair; one milk house 12 feet square, the weather boards very much decayed; one new log'd corn house 12 x 6 feet; one old tobacco house 40 x 22 feet, the weather boards want repairing and a new cover; 100 bearing apple trees, a small peach orchard and some cherry trees; about 90 acres of land inclosed in middling fence and other fencing necessary. The rent valued at 400 pounds of tobacco yearly exclusive of the widow's thirds and quitrents. The guardian permitted to get timber for repairs and to clear one acre per year.

234. 28 August 1747 Dr. John Smyth and Charles Connor, qualified by Joseph Sudler to view and value the property of Mary and Elizabeth Evains, daughters of the late John and Sarah Evains of Kent Island, deceased - on 18 July 1747 entered and found one dwelling house, 20 feet long with a brick gable end and a shed the whole length of the house with a brick chimney, with plank floors above and beneath, a brick cellar under the dwelling house, in tolerable good repair; a kitchen 16 x 12 feet with a brick chimney in tolerable repair; one 30 foot tobacco house in good repair; two out logg houses, 20 feet long each, in tolerable repair; one 40 foot tobacco house and one logg corn house wanting repair; an old 30 foot tobacco house and an old corn house worth repairs; 1,285 pannells of very old fence, the greater part rotten; 50 apple trees and some cherry trees. The guardian to clear all woods within the fence and a small skirt of woods without the fence, with timber for repairs; the rent valued at 1,100 pounds of tobacco per year.

234. 30 March 1747 - 28 August 1747 Thomas Marsh of Kent Island, Gentleman, to Robert Blunt of Kent Island, Planter - a bond of ₤100 to assure that a certain land mark will remain at the head of Martain's

234. Creek. Wits: James Sudler, Jo^n. Smyth, William Osburne, Samuel Wright.

235. 28 August 1747 John Granger of Kent Island, Planter, to Robert Blunt - a bond of ₤100 to assure a permanent land mark at the head of Martain's Creek. Wits: James Sudler, Jo^n. Smyth, William Osburne, Samuel Wright.

235. 9 September 1747 - 16 September 1747 Thomas Hynson Wright, Gentleman, to William Hopper, Gentleman - a division of a parcel of land conveyed to them by William Bishop, 18 August 1746 - part of "Smith's Mistake," then in his possession. Hopper receives 225 acres of land as his part. Acknowledged before Charles Downes and Nathan Wright.

236. 16 September 1747 William Starkey to his granddaughter, Ann Starkey Cole - gift of a negro girl named "Rose," aged five or six years - to be delivered at her day of marriage or at age twenty-one years. If Ann should die without issue then "Rose" to go to his granddaughter Sarah Cole, sister of Ann Starkey Cole, with all of her issue. If the first child of negro "Rose" shall live to age three years, it is to go to Mary Cole, sister to Ann S. and Sarah Cole. Acknowledged before Robert Lloyd and Nathan Wright.

237. 12 September 1747 - 1 October 1747 William Docwra, Planter, to James Hammond, Planter - consideration ₤60 current money and 13,000 pounds of tobacco - 172 acres, part of "Moor's Hope Addition" - adjoining "Miss Hitt," formerly surveyed for Stephen Rich, on Chestnut Hill Branch of Corsica Creek. William and Mary his wife (she being first privately examined) acknowledged before William Hopper and Nathan Wright. Alienation fine, six shillings, eleven pence sterling, paid to Richard Tilghman.

239. 12 June 1747 - 1 October 1747 John Davis, Jr., son of Thomas Davis, Planter, and Esther his wife, to John Davis - consideration ₤110.15.0 current money - 150 acres called "Peter's Lott," lying on Gravely Branch of Corsica Creek near a great pond. Acknowledged before N^n. Wright, Jr. and William Clayton. Alienation fine, six shillings sterling.

240. 14 August 1747 - 1 October 1747 John Collins to John Sertaine - consideration 3,000 pounds of tobacco - 290 acres, "Smith's Range Addition," lying on the Southeast Branch of Chester River - adjoining "Ripley," formerly laid out for Stephen Tully; the land laid out for Thomas Collins; "Smyth's Range." Acknowledged before James Brown and Humphery Wells, Jr.

241. 2 September 1747 - 1 October 1747 Nathaniel Scott, Planter, to Benjamin Covington, Planter - consideration 9,000 pounds of tobacco and ₤5 current money - 100 acres, part of "Tom's Fancy Enlarged," devised to him by his father Nathaniel Scott, deceased. Wits: Nathan Samuel

241. Turbutt Wright, Thomas Wright. Acknowledged before Thomas Hynson
Wright and Nathan Wright. Alienation fine, four shillings sterling,
paid to Richard Tilghman.

242. 9 September 1747 - 12 October 1747 William Hopper to Thomas Hynson
Wright - 220 acres, a division of the land they purchased of William
Bishop, part of "Smith's Mistake." Acknowledged before Charles
Downes and Nathan Wright.

243. 7 September 1747 - 12 October 1747 Thomas Hynson Wright to Nathan
Samuel Turbutt Wright, heir at law of the said Thomas - certain land
on the Deep Branch of Hynson Town Creek - adjoining Thomas Hammond
(no acreage given) - Nathan Samuel Turbutt Wright to dock and make
void the 'intail' of two tracts called "Warplesdon," 300 acres, and
"Solomon's Friendship," 100 acres, devised by Thomas Hynson's father
to him and his heirs forever entailed. Acknowledged before William
Hopper and Nathan Wright.

244. 7 September 1747 - 12 October 1747 Thomas Hynson Wright to Thomas
Wright - consideration ₤100 current money to be paid to Sarah Wright,
granddaughter of Thomas Hynson Wright - a parcel of land on Deep
Branch adjoining Thomas Hammond - running to Holton's Creek (no acreage given). Acknowledged before William Hopper and Nathan Wright.

245. 12 October 1747 Solomon Kenting, Planter, to James Kenting, Planter -
division of 200 acres of land, part of the 300 acres of land belonging to William Kenting called "Upland" - formerly in Talbot County
but now in Queen Anne's in the fork of Choptank River, adjoining
"Poplar Ridge Addition." (Metes and bounds of the division given
but no acreage.) Wits: Giles Hicks, James Payne. Acknowledged at
the County Court in Queens Town before Robert Lloyd and Associates.
Richard Tilghman, Clerk.

247. 17 October 1747 Thomas Lane of Talbot County and Mary his wife, to
James Tilghman of Talbot County, Attorney at Law - consideration
7,000 pounds of tobacco - all claim by virtue of will of William Clayton, late of Talbot County, to "Cole's Banks" and "Cole's Banks Addition." Thomas and Mary (she being first privately examined out of
his hearing) acknowledged before Robert Lloyd and William Tilghman.

248. 17 October 1747 Thomas Fisher and Hawkins Downes, appointed and sworn
by Jonathon Nicols to value the land of Joshua Clark, deceased - on
18 July 1747 entered into the land and found one framed dwelling house
not finished, 40 x 18 feet, which wants covering; one other dwelling
house lapt work, 20 x 15 feet with a shed 8 feet wide on one side, in
bad repair; one logg house, 20 x 15 feet in good repair; one other
logg house, 15 x 10 not worth repairing; a framed house, 30 x 15 feet
in good repair; a framed milk house, 8 feet square in good repair; a
new corn hosue, 20 x 6 in good repair; two tobacco houses, 40 x 20
feet and 35 x 22 feet, both in good repair; one tobacco house, 30 x
20 feet in bad repair; a tobacco house, 35 x 20 feet in bad repair;
one tobacco house, 35 x 22 feet in bad repair. 250 apple trees; the

248. fencing in good order. The guardian ordered to repair the houses and if she continues until the orphan is twenty-one to pay a rent of 450 pounds of tobacco yearly plus quitrents. If the orphan is removed from her charge, she is to pay 1,200 pounds of tobacco yearly with the quitrents. The guardian to clear 100 acres of land.

249. 23 October 1747 - 27 October 1747 Mary Powell of Kent County, Widow, and Ann Ivy of the same county, Spinster, daughter and heiress of Robert Ivy late of Kent County, to William Campbell, Planter - consideration 1,000 pounds of tobacco and ₤3 current money - 74 accres, part of "Reason" - lying on the west side of Thomas's Branch, adjoining "Prouse's Park" and part of "Ditteridge," in the possession of William Campbell. Wits: Charles Browne, Priscilla Browne, John Welch. Acknowledged before Charles Browne and Nathan Wright. Alienation fine, three shillings sterling paid to Richard Tilghman.

251. 24 August 1747 - 4 November 1747 Samuel Massey of Kent County, Hatter, to William Dames of Chester Town, Merchant - consideration ₤67 - 50 acres, part of "Poplar Hill," purchased of Morgan Ponder. Samuel and Sarah his wife (she being first privately examined) acknowledged before Charles Hynson and Beddingfield Hands, Justices of Kent County; certified by James Smith, Clerk. Alienation fine, one shilling sterling.

253. 23 June 1747 - 4 November 1747 John Dempster, Gentleman, to William Dames of Chester Town, Merchant - in exchange for a parcel of land in Cecil County lying on the west side of St. Thomas's Branch, Boheama Back Creek - 193 acres called "Bolding's Rest" heretofore conveyed by Thomas and Richard Bolding to the aforesaid William Dames - conveys two parcels of land on Jones's Creek - part of "Sheperd's Fortune," formerly conveyed by William Sheperd to Dempster - adjoining Thomas Hackett's part (no acreage given) - also a slipe containing 18 acres of land between Thomas Hackett and George Primrose's parts of "Sheperd's Fortune." Acknowledged before Charles Hynson and Bedingfield Hands; certified by James Smith, Clerk of Kent County. Alienation fine, two shillings, eight pence sterling.

254. 13 October 1747 George Mattershaw, Planter, in consideration for the education of youth and further that William Hopper and Christopher Cox hath built a dwelling house for a schoolhouse upon part of "Jamaica" - gives one acre of land on a branch near his house for the use of the schoolhouse and no other. Acknowledged before James Brown and Nathan Wright.

255. 6 November 1747 - 24 November 1747 William Dames of Chester Town, Merchant, to Thomas Marsh, Gentleman - consideration ₤360 current - two parcels of land, parts of "Sheppard's Fortune," one containing 248 acres and the other the slip between Thomas Hackett and George Primrose, containing 18 acres. William and Lucy his wife (she being first privately examined) acknowledged before William Hopper and Nathan Wright. Alienation fine, ten shillings, eight pence sterling.

257. 24 November 1747 Thomas Swan, Planter, and Sarah his wife, to his
son, Thomas Swan, Jr., Planter - a gift of 50 acres of land, part of
"Jump's Chance" - on the east side of Tuckahoe Creek on the east side
of the main road and adjoining "Jump's Choice" and the land William
Jump gave his daughter, Elizabeth. Wits: Jonathon Nicols and James
Downes, Jr. Thomas and Sarah (she being first privately examined)
acknowledged before William Hopper and Jonathon Nicols. Alienation
fine, two shillings sterling paid to Richard Tilghman.

258. 6 November 1747 - 24 November 1747 William Dames of Chester Town,
Merchant, to Thomas Marsh, Gentleman - consideration ₤25 current -
50 acres, part of "Poplar Hill," lying on the east side of a swamp
lying between the main road to Kings Town and a plantation (part of
"Poplar Hill") in the possession of Violet Primrose. Acknowledged
before William Hopper and Nathan Wright. Alienation fine, two shillings sterling.

260. 11 September 1747 - 24 November 1747 Margaret Coleman of Talbot County, Widow, to her daughter Elizabeth Coleman - one-half of 100 acres,
part of "Royston," purchased of Thomas Wilkinson, deceased, by George
Ayer, father of Margaret Coleman. Acknowledged before William Thomas
and Thomas Bullen, Justices of Talbot County; certified by John Leeds,
Clerk. Alienation fine, one shilling sterling.

261. 19 September 1747 - 25 November 1747 Thomas Carman and James Carman
to Solomon Seeney - consideration 7,650 pounds of tobacco and one
pistole - 100 acres called "Bradford's Addition" - lying on Elliott's
Branch, adjoining "Bradford." Acknowledged before Humphery Wells,
Jr. and Nathan Wright. Alienation fine, four shillings sterling.

262. 14 November 1747 - 25 November 1747 Dr. John Jackson to Christopher
Cox and James Cox, his son - lease of one acre of land, part of
"Smithfield's Addition," adjoining Thomas Wilkinson's dwelling house.
Term of lease is twenty-one years; not to keep store there or purchase
any goods not conveniently moved to their dwelling plantation or a
landing when sold. The privilege of moving their building to other
land extended. The rent is one fat goose yearly delivered at the
Doctor's house every year on 1 January. Acknowledged before William
Hopper and Nathan Wright.

263. 26 October 1747 - 26 November 1747 Ann Ivy, daughter and heiress of
Robert Smith Ivy, son and heir of Anthony Ivy and Ann his wife, daugh-
ter and heiress of Robert Smith, Esquire, deceased and Mary Powell,
widow and relict of the aforesaid Robert Smith Ivy, to Thomas Shoe-
brook - consideration 2,000 pounds of tobacco - 100 acres called
"Stoke" - lying near Elliott's Branch of Island Creek - adjoining
James Kersey's land, "Low's Arcadia." Acknowledged before William
Hopper and Nathan Wright. Alienation fine, four shillings sterling.

264. 26 November 1747 John Starkey, Planter, to William Bancks, Merchant -
consideration 3,000 pounds of tobacco - 50 acres called "Starkey's
Folly," in the woods near the head of Choptank River and adjoining

264. "Swift's Folly," now possessed by Ralph Swift, Jr. Acknowledged before Charles Downes and Jonathon Nicols. Alienation fine, two shillings sterling, paid to Richard Tilghman.

266. 27 November 1747 John Smith and Charles Connor, appointed and sworn by Joseph Sudler to view and value a plantation on Kent Island called "Sillin" - one-third part being the property of Ann Price, daughter of Andrew and Sarah Price of Kent Island - on 13 November 1747 entered into the plantation and found one 20 foot dwelling house with a brick gable end and 'chimley," a brick seller underneath, a shed the lenth of the house with a brick chimley in tolerable repair; a kitchin 16 x 12 feet with brick chimley in good repair; two logg houses, 20 feet in lenth in tolerable repairs; one corn house, wanting repair, also another corn house not worth repairing; a 30 foot tobacco house and a 40 foot tobacco house, wanting repairs; about 40 apple trees and some cherry trees; 1,285 pannells of fencing, old and rotten. The value of one-third of the plantation is 366 pounds of tobacco and two-thirds of a pound per year.

****

SOME QUEEN ANNE COUNTY PATENTS

Thomas Hynson Wright's certificate for 2,100 acres of land called "Tom's Fancy Enlarged" - granted 24 October 1734. A resurvey of "Tom's Fancy," granted 4 April 1717 for 100 acres, with 2,000 acres of vacant land added - lying in Tully's Neck. The vacant land is without cultivation or improvements. (Patents E.I. #3 f.373)

"Tappahannah," 1,375 acres of land surveyed 19 October 1715, for Benajmin Shurmer - near the head of Tappahannah Marsh. Patent issued on 10 September 1716. (Maryland Rent Rolls, Vol. 12 f.448)

"Edinburgh," 1,074 acres of land surveyed 17 August 1719 for Gilbert Falconer. Lying in the forrest between the branches of Chester and Choptank Rivers. (Maryland Rent Rolls, Vol. 12 f.455)

"Hemsley's Brittannia," 600 acres of land surveyed for William Hemsley - between the branches of Wye River and Tuckahoe Creek. (Patents C #3 f.196)

"Hemsley's Arcadia," 1,030 acres of land surveyed 12 December 1688 for William Hemsley.

"Craney Neck," 400 acres of land on the Isle of Kent, laid out for Robert Hewett, 16 October 1651. Patent issued to Hugh Lee and Hannah, his wife (Hannah, the widow of Robert Hewett). (Patents ABH f.143)

"Davis's Range als Wrexham," 600 acres of land surveyed for John Davis, 6 April 1685 - south side of Chester River on the south side of Red Lyon Branch in the woods. Possessed by Capt. John Davis of Talbot County. (Maryland Rent Rolls, Vol. 12 f.401)

QUEEN ANNE COUNTY, MARYLAND, LAND RECORDS

"BRADBOURNE'S DELIGHT" 337
BRADBURY
  Edmond 410
"BRAMPTON'S ADDITION" 266, 281
"BRANFORD" 519, 531
BRERETON (BREWTON), ENG. 227, 410
BREREWOOD
  T. 468
BRIDGEWATER, ENG. 227, 231
"BRISTOL MARSH" 525
BROAD COVE 257
BROAD CREEK LAND 459
BROADRIBB
  John 482
BROADRIB'S BRANCH 329, 379, 380
BRODAWAY
  Anne 207
  Nicholas 202, 207
"BROOMELY LAMBETH" 371
"BROTHERHOOD" 279, 365, 404
BROWN(E)
  Charles 500
  Edward 221, 309, 367, 437
  457, 481, 515
  James 202, 235, 240, 246
  248, 249, 255, 260, 262, 269
  270, 272, 279, 292, 294, 295
  298, 302, 303, 307, 312, 315
  317, 319, 327, 335, 342, 361
  362, 363, 365, 372, 382, 383
  384, 400, 401, 426, 428, 437
  439, 444, 448, 460, 461, 463
  473, 478, 481, 499, 506, 512
  517, 521, 522, 529, 532, 533
  John 220, 253, 264, 376
  Mary 221, 437
  Sarah 481
  Sarah (Mrs. Hawkins) 221
  William 411
BRYANT
  William 538
BRYDGES
  William 411
BUCHANAN
  Geer 468
  James 144, 309, 319, 326
  392, 433, 463
BUCK
  George 214, 229, 296, 297
  538, 539, 540
BULLEN
  Rachel 445

BULLEN
  Thomas 313, 374, 445, 508
BURCH
  Christopher 364
  Joseph 364
BURK
  John, Jr. 397
  John, Sr. 397
  Margaret 397
BURTHALL
  Earle 408
BUTCHER
  John 227, 231
BUTLER
  Thomas 326, 327

CALDER
  James 523
CALVERT
  Charles 315, 517
CALVERT COUNTY, MARYLAND 285
"CAMBERWELL" 532
CAMPBELL
  William 389, 478
  William, Jr. 272
CANNON
  William 272
CAPELL
  John 415, 416
CAREW
  Thomas 227, 231
"CARIGE" 256
CARDIFF, ENG. 413
CARMAN
  William 380
CARMICHAEL
  William 499
CARPENTER
  John 368
  John, Sr. 368
  William 370
CARROLL's COVE (WYE RIVER) 424, 443
CARTERET COUNTY, N. C. 518, 519
CARTER
  Henry 351
  Jacob 351
  Margaret 506
  Valentine 351
"CARTER'S FORREST" 395, 402
CARWITHEN
  Edmund 414

DOUGLIS
    Archable 240
"DOVER" - a horse 447, 465
DOWDALL
    John 249
DOWDNEY
    Nathaniel 414, 538, 540
    William 538
DOWNES
    Charles 203, 206, 208, 211
    212, 293, 296, 297, 305, 329
    330, 340, 343, 358, 359, 387
    391, 404, 406, 421, 441, 448
    453, 497, 502, 517
    Edward 481
    Frances 395, 402
    Henry 395, 402
    John 343, 395, 398
    John, Jr. 305
"DRAGON" - a horse 465
DREWY
    William 539
DUDLEY
    Elizabeth 518
    John 518
"DUDLEY'S DESIRE" 471
DULE
    Richard 232
DYKE
    Edward 227
DYSON
    Edward 231

EARLE
    James 329, 340, 377, 382
    James, Sr. 486
    John 255, 288, 302, 307, 320
    321, 327, 338, 339, 342, 361
    362, 368, 372, 377, 379, 383
    393, 400, 401, 420, 428, 434
    437, 438, 444, 447, 457, 459
    461, 504, 506, 513
    Margaret (Mrs. Cox) 329
EASTERN BAY 257
EDGERS
    John 214
EDMONDS
    Joel 410
EDMONSTON
    James 482

EDWARDS
    Anne (Mrs. Jacobs) 404
    William 404
ELBERT
    Frances 318, 499, 535
    William 535
ELICE
    William 312
ELIMAN
    Thomas 416
ELLIOTT
    John 234
    John, Sr. 351
ELLIOTT'S BRANCH 374
ELLIS
    William 312
ELSTON
    Roger 401
ELTON
    Jacob 412, 417
EMERSON
    John 395, 402
EMORY
    Ann(e) 277, 537
    Arthur 525
    Arthur, Jr. 376
    John 277, 537
    John, Jr. 256, 260, 298, 370
    Sarah 256
    William 537
    William, Jr. 277
ERICKSON
    Charles 459
    John 459
"ESTHER" 497
EUBANKS (HEWBANKS)
    William 223, 372
EUSTACE
    James 486
EVANS
    Thomas 410
EVERET
    Lawrance 338
EVERY
    John 538
EVITT
    Nathaniel 482
"EXCHANGE" 253
EYLER
    John 408

103.

JUGLET
Caleb 229, 232, 417, 539
JUMPE
Susanna 509
Thomas, Jr. 509
William 217, 256, 257, 275
341, 350, 365, 440, 471, 472
474, 479, 485, 486, 488, 491
495, 500, 509, 512, 519, 531
"JUMPE'S CHOICE" 244, 509
"JUMP'S LANE" 471
JUNIPER als JENIFER
249
JURDAN
Elizabeth 397
William 397

KAMBLY
Francis 414
KEMP
Baldwin 303
"KENDALL" 240
"KENT" - a ship 538, 540
KENT COUNTY, DELAAWARE 248
370, 466
KENT COUNTY, MARYLAND 204
242, 309, 310, 312, 320
321, 361, 362, 372, 382
423, 459, 476, 503, 516
KENT ISLAND 259, 338, 341
348, 459, 468, 500, 510
KENT
William 305
KERSEY
James, Sr. 379, 380
Thomas 379, 380
KERSLAKE
William 539
"KILLCRAY" 472
KILLIAM
John 414
KING
Alexander 254, 381
Mary 381
KINGDOM OF GREAT BRITAIN 491
KINGS TOWN (KINGSTOWN), MD. 215
217, 295, 342, 361, 362, 382
400, 401, 418, 421, 439, 439
460
KNATCHBULL
Mary (Mrs. Tuit) 346

KNATCHBULL
Robert 345, 346
KNIGHT
Annis 476
S. 423, 476, 523
KNOTTS
James 495
Nathaniel 393
Susannah 393
KNOWLES
James 506
"KNOWLES' RANGE" 323

LAMAN
Phillipa 232
"LAMBETH" 423, 476
"LAMBETH FIELDS" 345
LANE
Thomas 377
Walter 206
LANVAIR-YBRIN (ENG.) 410
"LARGE RA(I)NGE" 282, 485, 488
"LARGE RANGE ADDITION" 275
"LARRINGTON" (LARINTON) 249, 482, 504
LASKEY
John 538
LAURE
Mary 409
LEE
Jane 272, 274
John 532
Nicholas 414
Richard 272, 274, 498
LEE (LEY, LLEY)
Thomas 229, 411, 417, 482, 537
Thomas, Jr. 411
LEEDS
John 313, 374, 445, 450, 508
LEGG
John 410, 500
LEMAR
Charles, Sr. 286
LEONARD
John 252
LETCHMER
Gridmore 415
LEWIS
Dorothy 413
John 413
Maud 410
LIEGE 345

MERIDITH
  Thomas 307
MERRY
  Mary 538
  Samuel 538
MILLER
  Eliza 423
"MILLFORD" 252
MILLIS
  James 386
  Jane 386
"MIST HIT" (MISS OR HITT) 351
MITCHELL
  Francis 456
MOFFETT
  John 240
"MOLL, THE ELDER" 260
MONMOUTHSHIRE, ENG. 410
MOODY
  James 274
MOOR
  Charles 498
"MOORE'S HOPE" 354
"MOOR'S HOPE ADDITION" 351, 356
  358
MOOTH
  Thomas 225
MORGAN
  John 530
  Richard 415
  William 413
MORRIS
  William 412
MOUNTICUE (MOUNTAQUE)
  William 223, 224
"MT. HOPE" 513
"MT. MILL" 389
MULSE
  Thomas 415, 416
MURPHY
  Eleanor 500
  William 500
"MUSKETO RIDGE" 363

NABB
  John 440, 441, 447
  465, 466
"NAN" 447, 465, 497
"NANN" 240
"NANNY" 406
NEALE, Charles 407

NEALE
  Henry 346
NEALL
  Edward 508
"NEGLECT" 367, 515
NEVILL
  Anne 295
  John 217, 295, 426, 448, 532
NEW CASTLE COUNTY, DELA. 370
NEWCOMBE
  John 414, 538, 540
  William 538, 540
NEW GARMINN, ENG. 408
"NEW LONDON" 486
NEWNAM
  Daniel, Jr. 368
  Joseph 529
  William 456
"NEW READING" 387, 391, 502
NICHOLS
  James 523
"NICHOLSON'S VENTURE" 321
NICHOLSON
  John 321
"NOBLE'S RANGE" 395, 398
"NORREST'S ADDITION" 420
NORTH CAROLINA 518, 519
NORTHCOTT
  Sir Henry 411, 539
"NORTHUMBERLAND" 499
"NOTLAR'S DELIGHT" 216, 327
"NOTLAR'S DESIRE" 365, 404
"NOTLEY'S DELIGHT" 306
NUETT
  Robert 415, 416

"OAKEN THORP" 377
OGLE
  Samuel 315
OGLETOWN 220, 255, 294, 444, 457
OLDHAM
  Anne 253
  Edward 253
  John 500
"OLDSON'S RELIEF" 500
"OLD TOWN" 223
OLDTOWN 445
ONSLOW COUNTY, N. C. 518, 519
OSBURN
  William 510
"OUTRANGE" 279, 383

113.

QUEEN ANNE COUNTY, MARYLAND, LAND RECORDS

MARSH
William 52
"MARSHY CREEK" 29
"MARINA" 160
MARTEN (CAPT.) JOHN 169
MARTINGALE
Thomas 200
MARTAIN'S (MARTIN'S) CREEK (KENT IS.)
203, 234, 235
"MARTAIN'S (MARTIN'S) NECK 62
"MARY" - a ship 2
"MARYLAND MERCHANT" - a ship 169
"MARY'S CHANCE" 84
MASON
Anne 162
William 162
MASSY (MASSEY)
Katherine 137
James 64, 137, 228
Jane 137
Nicholas, Sr. 137
Peter, Jr. 137
Peter, Sr. 137
Rachel 137
Sarah 130, 251
Samuel 73, 125, 128, 129, 130
152, 251
"MASSY'S HAZARD" 137
MATTERSHAW
George 254
MATTHEW SMITH'S COVE (WYE RIVER)
59
MC CONNIKIN
John 197
Mary 197
"MC CONNIKIN'S FORTUNE" 197
MC COSH
Samuel 33
MC COYE - see Maccoy
MC GUIRE
Patrick 170
MC KITTRICK
Andrew 19
MEAD
William 175
MEADS
John 173, 174
MELOYD
Thomas 180, 188
"MIDDLE PLANTATION" 193

MILLBOURN
(CAPT.) JOHN 19
MILLER
John 71, 186
Michael 89
"MILL RANGE" 132, 134
MILLS
David 10
"MINK" - a horse 32
"MISS HITT" 237
MITCHELL
James 19
"MITCHELL'S ADVENTURE" 135
MOLLINEAU
Richard 118
MOLLIS
John 122
MOORE
William, Jr. 142, 143
"MOOR'S HOPE ADDITION" 237
MORAY
Stephen 32
MORGAN'S CREEK (ALS WYE RIVER) 59
MORRIS
Robert 193
MOUNSEER
Thomas 149
"MOUNTHOPE" (MT. HOPE) 87, 99, 135
"MT. MALUCK" 41
"MT. MILL" 21, 193

NABB
John 29, 119
"NAN" 178
NEALE
Edward 158
"NEGLECT" 233
NEVIL (NEAVIL, NEVILL)
Anne 96, 97
John 96, 97, 114, 126, 130
"NEW BUCKBY" 69
NEWNAM
Benjamin 6
Bexley 228
Daniel 225
Hannah 6
John 225
Joseph 151, 228
Rachel 225
Sarah 228
William 228

124.

NOTE:

The names and titles in the Patent
and Rent Roll records which appear
on page 91 are NOT included in
this index.